YOU WRITE THE PROGRAM, CHAMP.

Solve the mystery of the deserted mansion. . . .
Inherit a block of downtown Honolulu. . . .
Hang ten on a surfboard. . . .
Match wits with a man whose mind works like a computer. . . .

What happens in this book is up to the choices you make page by page. You'll find over thirty possible endings, from silly to scary to surprising. And it all begins when your plane touches down in beautiful Hawaii. . . .

THE HAWAIIAN COMPUTER MYSTERY

Janet Bly

Illustrated by Paul Turnbaugh

Chariot Books

from David C. Cook Publishing Co.

With much appreciation
to Mark Collister,
one of the "whiz kids"
in the Silicon Valley

Chariot Books is an imprint of the David C. Cook
Publishing Co.
David C. Cook Publishing Co., Elgin, Illinois 60120
David C. Cook Publishing Co., Weston, Ontario

THE HAWAIIAN COMPUTER MYSTERY
© 1985 by Janet Chester Bly for the text and Paul
Turnbaugh for the illustrations.
First printing, 1984
Printed in the United States of America
89 88 87 86 85   5 4 3 2 1

Library of Congress Cataloging in Publication Data

Bly, Janet.
    The Hawaiian computer mystery.

    (A Making Choices Book)
    Summary: A national computer programmer
champ wins a free trip to Hawaii and becomes involved in a dangerous adventure. The reader makes
choices to decide the outcome of the plot.
    1. Plot your own stories. 2. Children's stories,
American. [1. Mystery and detective stories. 2. Plot
your own stories] I. Turnbaugh, Paul, ill. II. Title. III.
Series.
PZ7.B6273Haw 1984   [Fic]   84-17453
ISBN 0-89191-954-6

CAUTION!

This is not a normal book! If you read it straight through, it won't make sense.

Instead, you must start at page 1 and then turn to the pages where your choices lead you. Your first decision seems harmless enough—will you volunteer to do a newspaper interview, or head for an afternoon at the beach? But soon you may find yourself headed for some strange and even dangerous situations.

If you want to read this book, you must choose to
Turn to page 1.

The huge crowded jet slowly descends above the Honolulu airport.

Sonja Huckaby chatters beside you. "Now, what are the names of the guides we're supposed to meet? Oh, yes, there's Miss Dela Cruz and . . . ."

"Kikukawa," you say for the tenth time.

"Ki-kuk-a-wa." Sonja giggles. "I can't seem to program that in." She shoots you a warning glance. "No remarks, please."

"Hey, I did it!" Dan Estrada shouts to your left. You can hear the familiar zings and zaps and mechanical voice instructions coming from the Dynamos game in his lap. This three-dimensional game won for the three of you a national computer programmers competition sponsored by Teledynamics, Inc. Your prize? Three days of fun in the sun in Oahu, as well as the possibility of lifetime royalties if you choose to sign an exclusive contract with Teledynamics. The judges seemed impressed not only with your unusual 3-D graphics, but also with the lock system. So far no one, amateur or pro, has been able to break into the code to beat the game.

Dan hands his micro across to Sonja. "See if you can beat that!"

"Control-C, Dan! We're ready to land," she retorts.

Turn to page 2.
Turn to page 2.

You feel the soft thud and bounce as the wheels touch ground. After a smooth coast down the runway, you squeeze through the aisle and into the portable hall, each of you clutching your micros.

"Aloha! Welcome to Hawaii!" An almond-skinned girl with waist-length black hair waves at you. "I'm Myra Dela Cruz, one of your guides." She places leis of orchids and plumeria around each of your necks.

"Where's Ki-kuk-a-wa?" Sonja asks.

"She'll be right back. She was called to the phone."

A dark girl in a bright, flowered kimono rushes up to Miss Dela Cruz. "Myra, the big daily newspaper at Waikiki wants one of the kids for pictures and interviews. It will mean missing out on the beach and the surfboard contest, but I'll be glad to take them."

Myra frowns. "Wait a minute, Kikukawa. Mr. Isham told me to get his permission for any change in the kids' schedule."

"But, Myra, it will mean great publicity for Isham's Teledynamics Company. And, besides, they want us to go right now. Don't worry, I'll take full responsibility." She turns to the three of you. "How about it, kids? Which one of you will go?"

Choices: You're the first to volunteer (turn to page 6).

You let Dan and Sonja fight it out; you'd rather be out on the beach (turn to page 4).

"You can call me Myra," Miss Dela Cruz offers as she loads your luggage into her van. Dan has gone off with Kikukawa. As Myra drives through the crowded streets you notice the milling Chinese, Japanese, and Filipino residents, as well as hundreds of tourists of various nationalities. You feel you've just been plunked down into a foreign country, rather than a part of the United States.

"Lucky for you that you came today and not last week," Myra comments. "We had a pretty rough storm."

"Did you lose any roads or bridges the way we do back home?" you question, mostly for the sake of polite conversation.

"No, I don't think so," Myra replies, "except I did happen to hear that the bridge in the rain forest was washed out. No big loss though. It only takes you to the old haunted mansion."

Sonja lights up. "Did you say haunted mansion? Do you mean a real spook house?" When Myra nods, Sonja pries further. "Is there any way we could see it? Like, is there another way to get there or something?"

Myra hesitates, then admits slowly, "Well, there is a secret tunnel entrance that not too many people know about. . . ."

Choices: You remind Sonja that you've come here to learn how to surf (turn to page 9).

You know Sonja's still smarting about missing the Waikiki interview. You help talk Myra into going to the forest (turn to page 7).

Kikukawa helps you load your machine and luggage into the back of a jeep. In the driver's seat sits a blond, bearded man whom your guide introduces as her friend, Bert Brushjel. He grunts in your direction.

You ride in silence for about ten minutes. Then Bert takes a sudden turn off the highway onto a narrow side road. You notice signs to Waikiki pointing in the opposite direction.

"Uh . . . are we going the right way?" you ask Kikukawa.

"We're not going to Waikiki," she states. Then she clears her throat. "You explain, Bert."

"How'd you like a nice detour to the island of Molokai, kid?"

Turn to page 10.

Myra's van bumps along the rust-colored road. Sunlight barely peeps through the heavy foliage all around. You ask Myra about a snake you think you see slithering through the twisted, tangled vines.

"Sorry!" she says. "No snakes in Hawaii. You must have spotted a lizard."

You think to yourself that it was the snakiest-looking lizard you ever saw.

Just around a bend, under a natural arch of broad-leafed trees that dangle with thick moss, you pass a waterfall and come to a stop at the edge of a washed-out bridge. "Up that cliff is the mansion." Myra points to a ninety-degree sheer rock mountain. "I'll be right back," she announces. In a few moments she returns to say, "The tunnel is very muddy, I'm afraid. We'll have to look at the mansion from down here through the telescope."

Sonja stomps her foot. "But we came all the way out here just to look through the mansion. I don't care about a little mud. Can't we go, anyway, please? Please?"

Choices: You volunteer to keep guard over the telescope and van (turn to page 27).
You mutter something about ruining your brand-new pants and shoes as you follow after Myra and Sonja (turn to page 13).

B. J. gives you some quick tips. "Lie flat on the board. Paddle out to where you see the waves build. When a big one starts to move, paddle ahead of it as fast as you can. When you feel the wave carry you, stand up. Like this . . ."

B. J. stands on the board, arms outstretched. "Be sure to straddle the middle. Keep your weight on the front foot. Guide the board across the face of the wave by a shift of your weight. Got it?"

Sonja soon comes flying back to shore, smooth as can be.

"Sure," you say. "Let's go."

The crisp, cold water and breeze refreshes you, makes you feel daring. Your arms hardly ache as you swing them hard. Was that a lift? You pull up at the edge of the board and try to rise. Splash!

You tumble under the surging waters. Salt burns your eyes and throat. Your lungs feel as though they will burst. After a long, agonizing moment, you gasp fresh air. At the same time you realize that something slimy has entangled both your legs.

Choices: You holler for help (turn to page 45).
You struggle to reach your board and float back to shore (turn to page 14).

After you check into your hotel and change into beach attire, you hike with Myra and Sonja down to the shore. Myra immediately catches the attention of three male surfers. You have to admit that she looks pretty good in her orange-and-yellow striped suit—for an old lady of twenty-five, anyway.

"The waves are perfect today," a guy named B. J. calls out.

Myra turns to you. "Have you ever surfed?"

After Sonja shakes her head, you say, "Not really."

Myra scoots two fiberglass boards your way. You watch as B. J. shoots under a high, rolling wave and out the end as the water tunnel crashes.

"That looks easy!" Sonja says. "And fun!"

You pick up your board and swing it around to take a closer look. You feel a hard thunk and hear a wail. You turn to see that you've just knocked over a young boy.

"What a nerd," Sonja taunts as she races out to the water.

You lean over and help the boy stand up. "You all right?" you ask.

The boy stops sniffing long enough to accuse, "You smashed up all my clams."

Choices: You say, "Sorry," and run out to the water (turn to page 8).
You help the boy pick up his clams (turn to page 43).

"I'm supposed to be in Honolulu. We have an important demonstration to give Wednesday night in front of international representatives of Teledynamics. They're expecting us. . . ." You try to appear calm, but you're beginning to feel uneasy.

"If you cooperate, you'll get back in plenty of time for your meeting. Meanwhile, we very much need your services. Let's just say we're going to 'borrow' you for a little while."

"Who's 'we'?" you ask.

"It's a long story," Kikukawa says softly. "There's really no time to explain right now."

The gravel road turns to red dirt. As you bump along, a wide meadow opens before you and a helicopter comes into view. Just beyond the grove of kikui trees you've been following stands a man with a rifle.

Choices: You yank the steering wheel sharply toward the trees (turn to page 34).
You pretend to pass out in order to buy some time (turn to page 40).

You and Sonja creep through the vines out in the eery stillness. You hear a "whoosh" sound and turn around to ask Sonja about it. She's not there. She's gone.

You twirl around where you are and call her name. "Come on, Sonja," you say. "Stop playing games!"

Then you feel something tugging you. You're being pulled down by some magnetic force— right through the ground!

Turn to page 148.

You have no trouble renting a pail and shovel. The boy shows you where to dig. You discover dozens of half-buried clams in the clear water. Just as you pull up your first one, a voice booms out, "Hey, there!"

You both turn around to see a heavy man with gray hair and three tiers of leis around his thick neck. He points a cigar at you. "How would the two of you like to earn a fast fifty bucks? All you have to do is look alive and ride on my float in the parade for twenty minutes. It's all ready to go and I don't have enough riders to fill it up. We want to put in a good plug for my restaurant, The Orchid Hut. How about it?"

The boy shakes his head and goes back to clamming.

Choices: You turn down the offer and continue digging in the wet, clam-filled sand (turn to page 16).
You decide to go with the fat man (turn to page 17).

When you finally make it through the tunnel and up the stairs, you survey the damage. Your shoes look ruined and the bottoms of your pants are caked with red mud. You pull off your shoes and socks as Myra hands you each a snack of pineapple fritters and lichee nuts. The top of the waterfall provides cool drinks.

The decrepit mansion hugs the cliff's topside, surrounded by wild fields of orchids and red and purple bougainvillea. "It was built in 1900," Myra explains. "A wealthy *haole* mainlander used it as a vacation home. After his death, a son moved here and married an islander. The wife, Olawa, turned out to be *pilikia,* much trouble.

"She put some kind of spell on one of her children when he disobeyed. The boy almost died. The husband fled with the children back to the mainland. Olawa lived in the house for many years after that; then she disappeared. Some people claim she lives like a hermit in a cave on Molokai. Meanwhile, the house just sits here, abandoned."

Sonja claps her hands. "Oh, how exciting! A mystery woman and everything . . ."

You ignore Sonja. "But you don't believe that, do you, Myra? That she really put a spell on the boy and all?"

Turn to page 15.

B. J. and Myra help you pull the snaky vines from your legs. "Common, everyday seaweed," B. J. explains. Sonja has fun stomping on the watery bulbs and bursting them.

When you're able to stand up, B. J. pats you on the shoulder and confides, "Maybe you'd be better off to try bodysurfing first. Helps you get the feel of that balance."

But Sonja's soon pushing out for her second round. You grab your yellow eight-pounder and paddle out again. You feel the waters rise. You grit your teeth and pull up steady . . . steady . . . you're up!

Ohhh . . . you're down again.

Back at shore you don't say a word. Later that afternoon you come back out, alone, to practice with bodysurfing.

Choices: The next morning you tell Sonja and Myra you aren't feeling well. When they leave for the rain forest, you return to the beach for more practice (turn to page 48).

The next morning you ask Sonja to give you some pointers (turn to page 50).

Myra shrugs. "The islanders around here take it seriously. Most won't come near this place."

You walk through the musty rooms. Moss grows on the bannister and walls. Just as you begin to climb the stairs, you feel a crunch under your bare foot and a sharp pain on your ankle.

"You've been bitten by a scorpion!" Myra exclaims. "Don't worry, it's not a fatal wound. But you will be in agony for a while." She pulls out a first-aid kit from her purse. After she squeezes out the poison, she bathes the angry reddened ankle in ammonia. Sonja investigates the squashed scorpion.

"Oh!" she gasps. "It's got little babies all over its body." She stomps on a wiggly one.

"Watch out," Myra warns. "The stinger's in the tail." Myra examines your ankle. "I don't know how we'll get you back to the van. Do you mind waiting here until I can get some help? We're just twenty minutes from town. I'll be back in an hour."

She hands you a flashlight. "Just in case we should happen to get stuck and it gets dark. . . ."

"What? You're going to leave me?" you gasp.

"I'll be glad to stay here with the big baby," Sonja offers.

Choices: You swallow your pride and tell Sonja you'd appreciate her company (turn to page 18).
You insist on waiting alone (turn to page 20).

Before long, your pail overflows with clams. You sit down to rest and pull out a pocketknife. Before you've cut into five clams, you find a small, round treasure—a pearl. You discover ten in all.

Your young companion also has ten. You remember the hundred dollars in spending money you brought with you on your trip. You offer to buy the boy's share of pearls.

"Ten dollars each," he says.

Choices: **You jump at the bargain (turn to page 30).**
You tell him, "No way!" (turn to page 28).

"I'm Jim Mawae. All you have to do is put on a lei and hop on the float. Your bathing suit will be just fine."

You stop in front of huge flat trailer spilling over with pink and white orchid designs. On one end stands a replica of The Orchid Hut. A simulated palm tree is ringed by hula girls in shocking pink skirts and tops. About ten other kids of various ages sit around looking at the dancers. Just as you begin to climb up, Mr. Mawae stops you. "Wait! I need to get your name and address for insurance purposes."

You tell him your name. He looks up with a startled expression. "Say that again, real slow." When you do, he says, "Now, spell it." He scratches his head. "Well, well, would you believe that?" he says to no one in particular. Then he taps your nose with his pencil. "Be sure and see me after the parade. Have I got a surprise for you!"

Turn to page 22.

Two hours later Myra hasn't returned. Dark shadows fill the house and yard. Your ankle still throbs. With great caution on your part, and reckless abandon on Sonja's, you have searched the two main floors of the old house. You find a few more scorpions scurrying around, shoo away a few bats, and discover an interesting locked trunk with some carvings that look Polynesian. Outside the wind begins to howl and black clouds cover the sun.

Sonja doesn't find it quite as fun as she did. "What if Myra doesn't come back?" she asks.

"Don't be silly," you say with authority. "She'll be here any minute."

"But what if she isn't!" Sonja's voice has a touch of hysteria.

You decide that now's the time to find a waiting place, while you can still halfway see.

Choices: You find a comfortable place in the house (turn to page 26).
You decide to limp down to the stairs, so you can be out in the open (turn to page 11).

You follow the men out to a large black limousine.

Myra, B. J., and Sonja are still out on the beach, searching for you. You apologize for worrying them and introduce the men. Myra knows Mr. Kaona. He explains the situation to her, and she asks several questions.

"He's a very respected island lawyer," she tells you. "The property will be held in trust for you until you're of age."

"You're a millionaire!" Sonja cries. "We can go into our own computer business. Phooey on Teledynamics! How do you compute that on the old chip?"

You don't answer. You feel a sudden need to sit down somewhere.

THE END

Within moments after Sonja and Myra leave, the eerie calm makes you jumpy. You could kick yourself for not insisting that they let you try climbing down the stairs and through the tunnel on your own. In fact, that's what you decide to do right now. Might as well wait for them down at the road as up here in the creepy mansion. Maybe you'll even catch them before they leave.

Your ankle still throbs; you wince with every step. You decide you'll make better time by scooting on your bottom. But once outside the mansion, you start descending too fast and lose control. Your eyes widen as you frantically try to grab a bush, a vine, anything. No use. Over the cliff you go, tumbling and screaming all the way.

Turn to page 29.

After the parade, all the participants wait for their pay at The Orchid Hut. When Mr. Mawae doesn't show up right away, the cashier hands out the promised wages. You decide to stick around and follow up on Mr. Mawae's comment.

An hour later Mr. Mawae still hasn't returned.

Choices: You continue to wait for Mr. Mawae an hour more (turn to page 57).

You know it's getting late and no one knows where you are. You return to find Myra and Sonja (turn to page 41).

The tunnel is ankle deep in red mud, so you don't make very good time. As you trudge along, you think through what you'll do from here. This would be just the kind of story that would feed Sonja's overactive mind. You'd rather keep it to yourself until you understand what's going on.

However, if there was a man down there, he might be trying to steal the van. That would certainly present problems for the three of you.

As you near the stairs you can hear Sonja's voice. "Why do they call this a haunted mansion, Myra? Just because it's empty?"

Choices: You interrupt by shouting, "Myra! There's a man in your van!" (turn to page 39).

You suddenly feel silly and decide to go back to the van instead of bothering Myra and Sonja (turn to page 46).

You hardly know what to say. As a Christian you are certainly aware of the spiritual world. And you know that the Bible has some strong things to say against messing around with witchcraft and that stuff.

You try to put this all together. The challenge of unlocking a code excites you. But the mention of voodoo makes you uneasy. Who are these people anyway?

You take a quick glance at the suitcase in the backseat. Your secret lock program hides inside. You really need to get back by Wednesday night to present it to the Teledynamics representatives. But wouldn't they be even more impressed if you could tell them about this adventure?

Bert breaks into your thoughts. "A storm's coming," he yells. "We've got to leave right now."

Choices: You decide to go with these strangers (turn to page 42).
You tell Kikukawa and Bert that you're sorry, but it's out of the question. You must stay in Honolulu (turn to page 51).

Your chest heaves as you try to catch your breath. You have a clear view of the van from the spot where you collapsed. It looks empty. After a moment you chide yourself for being so easily frightened.

Even if there was a man in the vehicle, you tell yourself, it doesn't mean he meant to harm you. Maybe he was just trying to get a nap. Or maybe it was just a reflection from someone walking through the forest.

A touch of curiosity, as well as disgust with yourself, gives you the courage to investigate. You slowly walk back down the road to the van and peer inside. No one is in there. You search around in the trees and vines nearby. Nothing suspicious there.

Then Myra and Sonja come bursting out of the tunnel. "Are you all right? We heard a scream?"

With much reluctance, you tell them about the face. Sonja squeals with delight, but Myra's face has a determined look. "Sorry, kids, we're going back."

Turn to page 32.

You settle down upstairs in the room that holds the Polynesian trunk. From there you both have a window view of the front of the house, so you can watch for Myra. Also, this room has the only decent chairs—Victorian high backs with arms. "At least we may get some rest," Sonja says.

You spend most of the time jumping at noises and trying to calm each other down. Then Sonja sees something. "Look! A searchlight coming from the trail!"

There's more than one. Soon, you see four lights beside some shadowy figures.

Sonja opens her window and shouts, "Here we are! We'll be right down."

But then you're amazed to see the lights and figures turn to run the other way.

Turn to page 59.

You stand beside the van and take a good look around you with the lens. You're especially on the watch for snakes or other forest creatures. All you notice are some beautiful blue-and-yellow birds. After following a few playful ones with your eye for some time, you put down the telescope and contemplate whether to do some exploring. But you soon get an eerie feeling down your spine and think someone or something is staring at you.

You twist around quickly and find yourself face-to-face with a strange man, gazing at you from *inside* the van window.

Choices: **You run through the tunnel after Myra and Sonja (turn to page 23).**
You run screaming through the forest until you find a hiding place (turn to page 25).

You find Myra, B. J., and Sonja resting on the beach. You try to act as nonchalant as possible. Then you call B. J. aside.

"Look at these!" you whisper.

B. J. analyzes one of the gems and hands it back. "Yeah? What of it?" he says.

"You can't fool me. These are genuine pearls! I'm rich!"

"Yep, they're pearls all right, but completely worthless as far as any jeweler's concerned. They're dull. The pearls with that magical luster come out of oysters. You've wasted your time."

That night you feast on a scrumptious meal of fresh clams in a special sauce. *At least,* you rejoice to yourself, *I'm not out a hundred bucks.*

THE END

You wake up in a hospital with Sonja and Myra leaning over you. "What happened?" you ask.

Myra holds your hand. "You're a mass of bruises and cuts from the nasty fall over the cliff. No concussion, but the doctor wants you to stay here for observation overnight."

"The doctor said Myra had no business taking 'children' up there," added Sonja. "I just right out told him we were computer champs . . . and . . . actually, I was really scared, seeing you like that. We thought maybe you were . . ."

A nurse walks in and asks Myra to sign some papers. As soon as she leaves, Sonja leans over. "I prayed hard in the van that you'd be okay. That was my first time . . . you know, to really pray like God was real and cared."

Choices: **You tell Sonja that she need not have worried; you can take care of yourself (turn to page 35).**

You thank her for praying and give God credit for helping you (turn to page 53).

You greet Myra, B. J., and Sonja with the good news, trying not to gloat too much. Then B. J. appraises your afternoon's haul. "Sorry to disappoint you. They're pearls all right, but they're absolutely worthless. They don't have any luster at all. The only good ones are from sea oysters."

The young boy disagrees. "You don't know what you're talking about. My brother says different. Now where's my money?"

You fork over all the cash you brought with you and try to avoid looking at Sonja.

"But the good news is," Myra adds, "we can get the chef at the hotel to cook these up for us in his famous sauce. I can taste them already. Won't we have the freshest Hawaiian feast on the island tonight?"

Somehow you can't quite enjoy your hundred-dollar clams.

THE END

Back at the hotel you and Sonja wait in the dining room for Myra as she changes her clothes. You're trying to keep an eye out for Mr. Isham of Teledynamics, who will be eating dinner with you, too. Sonja is very quiet, which is unusual for her. You suspect she's up to something.

"Okay," you say, "What are you thinking about?"

She screws up her most serious face, the one she uses when she's about to unscramble a computer problem. "I've been going over it in my mind ever since we left."

"Left where?" you ask.

"The haunted mansion, of course. There's a mystery out there that needs to be solved."

"Don't be ridiculous. That face was just a figment of my imagination . . . I think. Anyway, whatever or whoever's out there is none of our business. And besides, Myra's going to take us to the beach tomorrow. When would we have time to solve any haunted house mysteries?"

"Tonight!" she says very low. "I had planned to go without you, but now that you've been so nosy, you're invited along."

"You're crazy! How would we get there? What could we possibly see at night? What will we tell Myra?"

"I've got it all figured out. Will you come with me?"

Choices: You refuse to have anything to do with it (turn to page 49).

You decide you'd better go along to see that she stays out of trouble (turn to page 52).

After the crash, Bert and Kikukawa appear to be knocked unconscious. You crawl over Bert and climb out of the jeep. You haven't time to check for injuries, for you hear feet running in your direction. You don't look back. You run as fast as your legs can go. About the time you feel you're going to drop, you discover a row of what look like oleander bushes.

You collapse for a moment behind them and listen. As far as you can tell, no one is still chasing you. All you can hear are the comforting noises of a bush highway nearby.

That's when you remember that your Dynamos locking code is still tucked into your suitcase in the back of that jeep. You're the only one who has a copy.

Choices: **You decide to sneak back to the jeep and retrieve your belongings (turn to page 44).**
You make a run for the highway in hopes of finding help (turn to page 47).

That night you can't sleep. Sonja's mention of prayer pricks at your conscience. As a Christian who accepted Christ several years ago, you have a fairly regular routine of Bible reading and talking to God. But ever since you won that computer contest, you've been so busy. . . . And besides, this has been a vacation for you.

"Forgive me, Lord, for neglecting you," you confess. "I'm the one who's been the loser. I've missed you."

On a hunch you lean over and pull open the nightstand drawer. You pick up the complimentary Bible inside.

You've been reading in the Book of Acts for almost an hour when the nurse walks into the room.

Choices: **You close the book quickly and slide it under the sheet** **(turn to page 127)****.**
You greet the nurse with a friendly hi and keep on reading **(turn to page 80)****.**

"Get moving over to that helicopter!" the man with the rifle orders.

"But what about the others?" you ask.

"They'll have to take care of themselves," he replies.

Once in the copter, the man starts the engine and guides the big bird up. You soon watch Oahu fall behind as you skim over the ocean. The man beside you doesn't say a word, so you use the time to investigate the array of sticks and pedals and instruments he's using. You also take a closer look at your companion. His dark complexion accents the graying hair. He wears several jade rings on his fingers and a jade stone around his neck.

You look away when he glares at you. That's when you notice the boat down below. Suddenly the copter makes a low swoop over the waves. You feel you could reach out and touch them.

Choices: You make a flying leap out of the helicopter (turn to page 56).
You fight the impulse and stay put (turn to page 77).

As you climb into the helicopter, Jade speaks abruptly. "Hey, Bert, it's the only way. We've got to get this thing figured out!"

Bert nods curtly, and says, "Don't worry about it now. We're all scared. Just no more strong-arm stuff, okay?"

Turn to page 42.

Kikukawa bites down on a fingernail. "About two weeks ago I began to notice that someone had been tampering with the machine. Then one day it was locked up tight. If I don't break the code, I'm stuck. Five years' work down the drain."

"What kind of computer do you have?"

"IBM personal computer with one megabyte of core memory . . . dual disk drives . . . ten-megabyte hard disk."

"How many users?"

"I'm the only one programming; no one else knows the first thing about it. Bert had a class or two at the university, but I'm the only one with actual experience."

You keep throwing questions to her as quickly as they come. Computer talk always stirs up your old adrenalin. "So there's no password? How about a modem? Are you on a time-share?"

"Come on, now. We're just an amateur operation—stuck out in the boonies all by ourselves. Far as I know, no one knows or cares about what we're doing." Then she stops. She looks intently at you as though she's trying to analyze something. Finally she asks, "Do you believe in voodoo?"

Choices: You try not to, but you can't help it; you laugh in her face (turn to page 60).
You don't answer her yet. You want to sort out your thoughts (turn to page 24).

Myra and Sonja dash back with you to the van. The three of you see nothing suspicious. No face. No one in the van.

"You just saw a reflection from the trees or something," Sonja teases. "Boy, don't you have an imagination!"

"It could have been a local out hiking or something," Myra assures you. "But in any case, I think we'd better head back to town."

"But we haven't seen the haunted mansion yet," Sonja protests.

"I'm sorry, kids. I'm completely out of the mood right now. But I'll make it up to you," she adds when she sees Sonja's face. "I'll take you to a scary movie or something tonight."

Sonja brightens. "Hey, that would be even better. There's probably nothing but a bunch of rats and bats in that old house anyway," she says as the three of you hop into the van.

THE END

You feel the jeep screech to a halt. Kikukawa gently shakes you as she says to Bert, "Now look what we've done. What's the point in these scare tactics? Can't we tell the kid what's going on?"

Bert lets out a long sigh. "You're right. But you'd think a computer champ would have more stamina. You explain the details when you see some signs of life. I'll go talk to Jade."

Slowly you open your eyes and see Bert standing next to the man with the rifle. Kikukawa assures you that she'll explain who they are.

She begins, "I'm an anthropologist and my main interest is the island peoples. I received a government grant about five years ago to gather information about ancient tribal customs. Bert and his friends belong to NO-GRO, a political action group interested in preserving the delicate geological balance of the islands. They learned of my project and have been invaluable in supplying me with people in the eastern wilderness areas of Molokai who had access to resources I didn't."

"But what does all that have to do with me?"

"I've been recording my findings on a computer. But lately I've had some strange problems."

Turn to page 38.

Turn to page 38.

As you cut through an alley, you stumble over something in your haste. You try to kick it out of your way. It just scoots in front of you, so you bend down to pick it up. It's a round, hard, white hat with a rim. The letters "J. R. Hitchcock" are engraved inside.

Choices: You toss the hat back down (turn to page 139).
You carry the hat with you (turn to page 64).

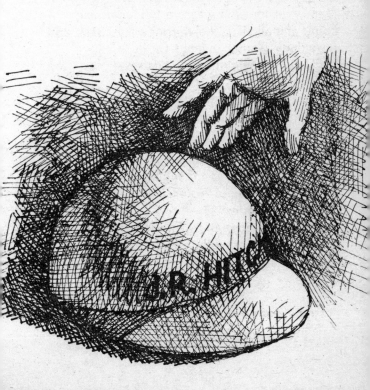

All of you settle snugly in the four-passenger helicopter. You sit in front with Jade, the pilot. Intrigued, you watch every maneuver he makes with the mechanical bird.

You pass over a town along the coast of Molokai. "Kaunakaki," Kikukawa tells you.

Suddenly a range of mountain peaks looms before you. You cross over some and settle down into a valley near a home built against the foot of a cliff. It looks well hidden and protected.

Kikukawa's unorthodox household consists of two male servants; Bert; Jade, the rifleman; a Maori warrior who wears a full-length cape of some animal skin; the warrior's son, Seki; and an elderly woman named Olawa.

"How is everything?" Kikukawa asks the woman.

"Not good. Mountain still angry. It rumbled all night," says Olawa.

Turn to page 54.

You watch Sonja and Myra wade out with B. J. as you pile clams in a pail.

"Where are my pearls?" the boy yells.

"What?"

"Oh, here they are." The boy grabs up three round objects and stuffs them in his pocket. "After a storm," he explains, "you find the ones with pearls. I'm going to be rich."

Choices: You decide to try a little clamming yourself (turn to page 12).
You figure the kid doesn't know what he's talking about. You go surfing (turn to page 8).

You scoot along through the trees until you catch a glimpse of the jeep. Bert and Kikukawa are stretched out on the ground.

A sudden crunch from behind startles you. "Don't move, kid!"

You turn to stare into the barrel of a rifle.

Turn to page 36.

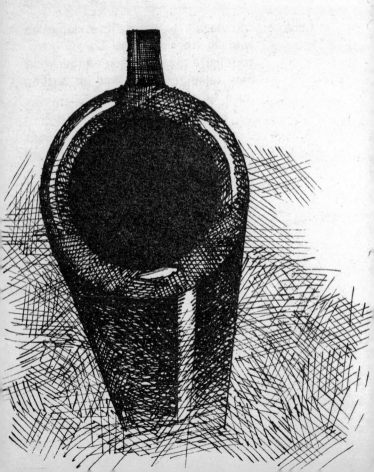

You continue to gulp water as you flounder in the waves. You panic as you try to imagine what could be wrapping itself around your legs. Just as you're sure you're going to drown, B. J. booms out close to your waterlogged ear, "Relax! I've got you!"

He drags you back into shore with ease. You can barely make out Sonja's face. She's peering at you with worried eyes.

"Watch out for my legs. Something's got me. . . ." you whisper.

You cringe when you hear Sonja's shriek of delight. "You've got yourself completely wrapped up in seaweed," she announces between laughs. "Sorry, but you do look hilarious."

After Sonja, Myra, and B. J. pull you loose from the seaweed, you admit you're worn out and would like to try clamming instead.

Turn to page 12.

At the other end of the tunnel you blink at the sunlight. You edge up to the van windows and peer in. No one is inside. You climb in to take a closer look around. The door slams shut behind you!

Then the van's engine turns over and the vehicle lunges forward down the road. You rush to the driver's seat and slam your foot on the brake. The pedal smashes to the floorboard, but the van keeps moving. All the doors are somehow locked up tight.

The steering wheel veers to the left off the main road and edges the cliff bottom. Without hitting a tree, you finally come to a stop on the other side of the cliff. You tell yourself the cold facts. Cars don't drive by themselves. However, the van turns a full circle and retraces the path back.

Just as you turn the corner towards the tunnel opening, you see Myra and Sonja waving you down.

"Would you please tell me what you're doing?" Myra demands.

Choices: **You feel foolish telling Myra the car drove itself, so you say you hot-wired it for the fun of it (turn to page 61).**
You tell the whole story about the face and the automatic driving (turn to page 63).

Once on the highway, you begin to thumb for a ride. No one stops for what seems like a long time. You're very hot, tired, and thirsty. If only you could have just one drink. . . .

A psychedelic painted van screeches to a stop beside you.

"Need a ride, kid?" A man with long hair and glazed eyes leers down at you. A sickeningly sweet smell reaches your nose. "We've got lots of eats and lots of treats. Just hop right in."

Choices: You decide to travel in the van just long enough to get refreshed (turn to page 119).

You say, "Thanks, but I'm waiting for a patrol car" (turn to page 134).

All day Tuesday you ride the waves . . . or try to, anyway.

And all day Wednesday.

On Wednesday afternoon, just before your computer program presentation, you have your own private show for Sonja. You hang ten all the way to shore.

THE END

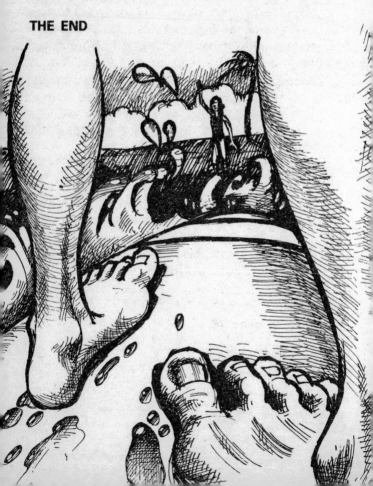

That evening after dinner you hear a knock at your hotel door. It's Sonja. "Are you sure you haven't changed your mind?"

"Are you going out there alone?"

"Well, no. I'm not going at all. When Myra told us about the note she got saying Kikukawa had car trouble, I figured they'd take care of it soon and Dan would go with me. Good old Dan. *He's* not afraid of adventures."

"It won't work, Sonja. You can't use that old trick to get me involved. I have no desire whatsoever to solve any mysteries about that haunted mansion."

Sonja turned to leave. "I guess I'll just wither away in my room watching television or something."

"Good-bye, Sonja," you say.

You're in the middle of working on your computer program presentation for the following night's ceremony, when the telephone rings. Myra sounds very relieved. "Thank goodness. I thought you both may have plotted something."

"What do you mean?"

"Sonja's disappeared!"

Turn to page 74.

"I'll be glad to help you," Sonja says with a pleasant smile. "Although I know it's been mostly luck with me getting up so fast. You'll catch on real quickly, I'm sure. However . . ." she says, with an I've-got-you-where-I-want-you look, "there is one condition. . . . This morning we'll hit the waves, and this afternoon . . . off to the haunted mansion!"

Turn to page 7.

You're surprised how cooperative Bert and Kikukawa are. They talk over some ideas, and then Bert tells Jade, the man with the rifle, that they're taking you back to your hotel.

As Bert reaches the jeep, Jade lifts his rifle and commands, "You're not going anywhere but into that helicopter—all of you!"

Choices: You make a mad dash for the highway beyond the grove of kikui trees, leaving Bert and Kikukawa between you and the rifleman (turn to page 47).
You walk with the others to the helicopter (turn to page 37).

You meet down in the lobby after Mr. Isham leaves and Myra goes to bed.

"Now what?" you ask.

"Just follow me."

You walk out into the brisk night wind. Sonja leads you to a little Chinese diner and introduces you to a broad-shouldered man in his twenties. "This is B. J.," she tells you. "He's a friend of Myra's. She told me about him while we were climbing the stairs today. He has his own ideas about what's going on out there at the mansion. He says he could use our help."

Turn to page 69.

"I know you go to church," Sonja continues, "but after a year of working together at the Dynamos project, I can't remember you talking about God. I think about him a lot lately. That's one reason I wanted to go to the haunted mansion. I thought maybe if we had personal contact with some of that magic, well . . . I could know he's for real."

You blush with shame. First, you regret not sharing your faith with your friends. Second, you're shocked to think Sonja wanted to find out about God by following after some hocus-pocus. You tell her now what you do know. "Sonja, as a Christian I know that you can never get to know God until you understand and believe in his Son, Jesus. He's a real-life, flesh-and-blood demonstration of God.

"Oh."

You sense Sonja's disappointment.

"But Jesus died a long time ago. I want something in black-and-white, something I can see and touch that proves God exists. I guess when it comes to spiritual things, I'm not even at BASIC."

Just then Myra walks back in. "Bad news, I'm afraid. Your scorpion wound has gotten infected. You'll have to stay in the hospital and miss the demonstration for Teledynamics."

Turn to page 35.

"What do you make of it?" Kikukawa prods the old woman.

"Eruption likely to come any day now."

You wonder how many other details like this Kikukawa has neglected to mention. She grabs you by the shoulder and steers you into a back room. You see the computer on a worktable. "When can you get to work?" she asks.

"Bring me something to eat, and I'll start right now," you reply.

She looks relieved as she sends a servant scurrying to the kitchen. "How will you go about it?" she asks.

"Well, I'm guessing that traditional methods are a good start. If you're as isolated as you say, your 'intruder' may not be up on the latest." You push some buttons, saying, "I'll try to break through by erroring out. Then I'll look for trap doors. If that doesn't do it, I'll go for a core dump. By the way, you don't happen to have a high-speed printer?"

She shakes her head.

You groan, "I have a feeling I'm going to be here awhile."

At that moment the green phosphorescent screen flashes a large 3-D graphic of a coiled, hissing snake! Kikukawa jumps up. "There it is! We must leave and warn the others! Quickly— you must not stay in here!"

Choices: You follow Kikukawa out of the room (turn to page 62).

You stay firmly in your place before the screen (turn to page 76).

Your ears feel as though they will explode as you struggle to surface. You're being tugged by a current. The good thing is that the current is pulling in the direction of the boat. The crew on board begin to cheer and throw long pieces of rope with buoys and life preservers tied to them.

You miss the first preserver. The next one you clutch with all your might with only one arm, while sea-hardy sailors tug and heave. Your other arm hangs useless at your side. Finally, your drenched body collapses on top of the deck. Despite the burning pains in your left arm and shoulder, you can hear the faint drone of a rotor's whir in the distance.

"Will they be back for you?" a man who looks like the captain asks.

"I hope not," you say.

"In that case, we'd better get you to a doctor. That arm looks broken. You're lucky, kid. You could have been killed."

Turn to page 58.

Mr. Mawae rushes in the back door with an elderly gentleman. He introduces you to Mr. Kaona, his lawyer.

"Sorry we took so long. I had to chase all over the island to find him. Thought maybe you'd be gone by now."

Then he tells you a fascinating story.

"The previous owner of The Orchid Hut died several years ago. Left no heirs. But the will stated that the property would be deeded over to the first person with the same first and last name who happened to walk into this restaurant. Do you have any identification?"

"Sure, back at the hotel, but—?"

"That's all you need. And I might add, the package includes nearly a block of prime Honolulu real estate."

"But that must be worth thousands. . . ." you sputter.

"Six and a half million dollars, to be exact," Mr. Kaona replies.

Turn to page 19.

58

After a somewhat comfortable ride, except for your aching arm, the boat docks at a resort-type place on the western end of Molokai. One of the crewmen returns after a brief visit ashore with a native. "The doctor's gone to the rodeo out on the plantation," the crewman reports.

"Rotten luck," the captain grumbles. "Well, how about it, kid?" He points to the native. "Manu can take you to the rodeo on the back of his motorcycle. I don't guarantee he'll get you there in one piece. But if you stay with me, we may not get you any medical attention until Maui."

Choices: You sail with the captain to Maui (turn to page 72).

You ride on Manu's cycle to the rodeo (turn to page 131).

"That must not have been Myra," Sonja says quietly. "Now what do we do?"

Before you can answer, you hear both of your names called. "Don't say anything!" Sonja cries. "That's not Myra's voice. Anybody could be down there!"

You hear your names repeated, this time louder and closer. "That's Dan!" you say. "I'm sure it is!"

"We're up here, Dan," Sonja yells through the window.

"Well, come out of there right now," he shouts back. You can tell he's half mad, or half scared. "If you think I'm coming in there after you, you're crazy!"

Soon the three of you are reunited. Dan explains that Myra had a slight accident on the way back to town. She saw a snake crossing the road, swerved to miss it, and tipped the van over. "She's all right," Dan quickly adds. "Just shaken up. Mr. Isham insisted that she rest at the hotel. He sent some of his workers with me to find you guys. Some help! The first noise out of you and they all ran back down the hill. Guess they thought you were ghosts."

"Well, you'll just have to go get them to come right back up," you say. "This 'ghost' needs to be carried. My 'spirit' ankle is complaining like real flesh and blood!"

THE END

Kikukawa opens the jeep door on her side and runs around the front to the driver's seat. She slips in under the wheel and backs the vehicle around. You hear several shouts of "Hey! Come back here!" behind you.

You sit in an uncertain silence as Kikukawa steers towards the highway. Then you say, "I'm sorry. I didn't mean to laugh—I really felt scared, and I didn't know what to say. As a Christian, I believe that stuff is real, but I don't want anything to do with it."

"Don't worry about it. All of a sudden I came to my senses. What a crazy idea all this is! We could be charged with kidnapping or worse, if this ever got out. Then the project would be ruined for sure. I don't suppose I could talk you into being quiet about the whole thing?"

Choices: You decide you'll keep the events of the past hour to yourself (turn to page 120).
You tell Sonja about it first chance you get (turn to page 135).

Myra fumes all the way back to the hotel. You can tell she's probably thinking, *Why did I have to get assigned to such brats?*

You determine you'll be as cooperative as you can for the rest of your Honolulu stay.

THE END

As Olawa shoos everyone out of the house, you and Kikukawa head for a cave at the north end of the canyon. "Do you have any suspects at all?" you prod.

"Well, Olawa knows all the ancient incantations. But she lost her husband and children when she cursed her son, Kainoa, in a fit of rage. Since then she's stayed away from the voodoo." Kikukawa stops a moment to shake a pebble from her shoe. "There is Kainoa. He appeared about a year ago and begged Olawa to tell him all the old magic. She refused. She says he wants to make her queen of the Islands—maybe the world. He'd be king, of course. A real nut."

"But, I don't understand. How . . . ?"

"Kainoa's a computer genius. He's broken into the most complex business programs. He used to feed the info into his own computer. Now he claims he can retrieve data straight into his own brain memory bank. That snake curse. . . . It's the same one Kainoa received from his mother as a child. Could be he's trying to pressure her, to show her he's getting the spells from some other source. Meanwhile, we stand to lose five years' worth of work." Kikukawa stops as you enter the cave.

Turn to page 66.

Sonja's face lights up. But Myra warns, "The island magic isn't something to play with. I'd better get you both back to town right now."

Myra looks back over her shoulder several times as she steers the van back to the highway.

"I've seen enough to know it's real," she continues. "The *Kahunas* talk to evil spirits. They even curse their enemies. I have a relative who has talked to the dead."

"But, Myra," you protest, "the Bible warns us to stay completely away from things like that."

"Isn't there any way to protect yourself?" Sonja interrupts.

Choices: You explain to Sonja what you know of Christ's power (turn to page 65).

You decide it's wiser to just change the subject (turn to page 144).

You put the hat on. As you turn the next corner, you hear some shouts and suddenly find yourself facedown on the sidewalk. A native has pinned your arms and legs. He jabbers in your ear, "Oe, Hitchcock, *hele mai. Wikiwiki, wikiwiki.*"

You know that *wikiwiki* means "hurry." The "Hitchcock" part reminds you of the hat. You try to explain you haven't stolen it and you're glad for him to have it back. In response, the man picks you up and carries you into a nearby gym.

As you protest and try to explain, boots are jammed on you, along with white breeches, knee guards, and a jersey. You're handed a long stick that reminds you of a croquet mallet, and a whip.

You say the only Hawaiian word you can think of at the time: *"Aole! Aole!* which means, "No! No!"

The man pays no attention to you. He takes you outside to a grassy court and sits you on a jet black horse.

Turn to page 68.

"Sure," you say. "When you invite Jesus, God's Son, to be your Savior, you gain at least two things. You have God as your personal, daily friend. And you have his supernatural help to do right and fight evil. You can tell the devil to leave you alone, in Jesus' name, and he has to do just that."

Sonja looks at you in a wistful way. "More than anything, I'd like to have God be my close friend."

Talking about Jesus so openly in front of Myra and Sonja has given you a new courage. You're surprised how easily the words continue to come out. "You can, Sonja. Just ask him. He doesn't turn anyone away."

As you get out of the van and walk up to the hotel lobby door, Myra softly touches your shoulder. You turn to see that her eyes are misty. "Thank you," she says.

THE END

"We'll be safe in here for the next hour. The screen image usually disappears by then. Later we'll return and you can work on the lock again. Meanwhile, you'll want to meet Olawa's friends, the volcano people." Kikukawa holds your hand in the inky blackness as you walk on a soft yet pebbly surface.

A light suddenly blinks on. Bert has a lantern of some kind in his hand. As you walk along you're startled to notice that the rocks beside you seem to be moving. You cry out when one very close to you suddenly spurts out in your direction.

"What's wrong with the rocks?" you screech.

Kikukawa laughs as everyone stops at a wide, clear place in the cave and sits down in various places. "The volcano people!" she answers. "They're checking you out to see who and what you are. Sit down and watch them. They won't hurt you."

As the lantern casts an eerie shadow, you stare at dozens of rock-shaped creatures. Some of them roll along. Others shoot out long tentacles and appear to walk on them or explore with them. You even see some roll straight up the cave walls and over your head!

Turn to page 73.

Soon a white ball flies your way, and so do about half a dozen uniformed riders on horses. An ivory-colored animal crashes right up against you.

Choices: You know how to ride a horse; you stay on (turn to page 123).
You've ridden a horse maybe three times in your life; you tumble to the ground (turn to page 140).

B. J.'s jeep bumps along as you and Sonja pull your sweaters tight around you in the chilly night air. B. J. screeches to a halt. "We'd better stop here and walk in," he announces. "Just in case . . ."

"Just in case what?" you inquire.

"I think there's some kind of gang holed up there. They may be armed, so we've got to be very careful. All I want to do is catch sight of them on the premises. Then I'll have something to go on to report to the police." B. J. leads the way through the dusky forest. Having him along makes the shadowy ferns and branches look less intimidating.

"We're going up the back side," Sonja whispers to you.

Sure enough, you hike up the back side of the cliff. You can see the mansion looming high above you. No lights or anything. Maybe there's no one here and you can all go home. . . .

Then the bottom falls out from beneath you. You feel yourself falling, falling. . . .

Turn to page 70.

The crazy thing is, you're falling forward, not down. You have the sensation of being sucked through tons of rock and dirt. Your head feels light, dizzy, as though you might faint or suffocate.

Suddenly you blink when the blackness turns to bright light. You sink to your knees into what looks like an ordinary living room. Sonja and B. J. drop in front of you.

A voice booms out: "What are you doing on my property at this time of night?"

As soon as your vision clears, you see a man standing before the three of you. He has dark hair, dark skin, and a trim, straight mustache. He's wearing a white, long-sleeved silk shirt with a purple vest and pants of some shiny material. He seems quite angry.

"Who are you?" B. J. booms right back. "This property belongs to the great Olawa. All Honolulu knows that."

"I am Olawa's son! I am Kainoa!" he says, as though he had just announced he was the King of Siam or something. And just at that moment he points his hand at B. J. An electric current shoots out from his fingers and B. J. disappears before your eyes!

Choices: You charge the man in self-defense
(turn to page 143).
You grab Sonja to try to shield her
(turn to page 75).

The captain and his crew leave you alone and tend to their business. You rest in a plush deck chair and try to relax your throbbing left arm in a comfortable position. Something soft and wet rubs against your good arm, startling you. You look down into the friendly brown eyes of a brown and white ball of fur. The puppy pumps its tail to greet you. You pat its head and say, "Hi, boy."

That's all the mutt needed. In the next instant he's up on your lap and pawing you. You let out a roar of irritation. The captain and a crewman come running.

The captain chuckles. "So, Pilikia's got you. He's still living up to his name: trouble." He swats at the pup. "Go on, get down. You're not wanted here."

Pilikia sulks behind a coil of rope. You feel sorry for complaining about him. "It's okay, captain," you say. "I was just worried about the arm. I'll keep an eye on him."

After the captain returns to the helm, you coax the puppy back. He runs around the deck chair and shows off with some somersaults. A shout interrupts the act. "Look out!" someone screams from behind, just as a huge surge of seawater crashes against the side of the boat.

Turn to page 98.

"Do they have eyes or ears?" you ask.

"Not in the human sense," Kikukawa says. "They're products of the inner volcanic atmospheric conditions. They thrive in darkness and heat and gaseous air best. But they love Olawa. Whenever she's around, they swarm down here in this cave."

You can tell that Bart and Jade aren't very crazy about the creatures. They keep shoving them aside. Jade even picks one up and throws it across to one of the servants. The "rock" spreads out dozens of tentacles and clings to the man. Then the long arms are sucked back in and the creature rolls down the man's body.

You're fascinated with these weird beings. You'd love to know more about them, but something happens next that astounds you all. A high-pitched sound rings out. It's unlike anything you've experienced before. It's very piercing to your ears, yet you sense that the sound has taste and smell and depth to it, too. The creatures begin to roll and run on their funny arms and scatter back down into the depths of the cave.

Olawa chases after them and you hear Kikukawa yell, "Olawa, where are you going?"

Choices: You follow Olawa and the creatures (turn to page 136).

You stay where you are (turn to page 78).

You and Myra search the hotel floors, and then take the elevator down to the dining room and lobby. You're just about ready to squeal about Sonja's plan to investigate the haunted mansion, when you spot Sonja. She's in the game room with a little boy.

Relieved, you scurry over just in time to hear her say, "It just can't be! How did you do that? It's impossible!"

"What are you up to, Sonja?" you demand.

Tears are running down her cheeks as she bawls, "Sammy unlocked our system!"

You take a good, hard look at this Sammy, while Sonja continues, "I was showing off our Dynamos game and telling about our lock, and he told me he could break into it. I dared him to try . . . and he did it!"

Sammy stares back at you with a proud, but not obnoxious, smile. Sonja pulls you aside. "But we don't have to tell the Teledynamics people. If we just keep quiet, no one will ever know. . . ."

Choices: You don't tell Teledynamics that the code has been broken (turn to page 126).
You admit to Teledynamics that the code is not foolproof (turn to page 146).

The man stands silent before you for several moments. You experience a strange pressure on your brain, a slight impression that your thoughts are being monitored. Then Kainoa speaks. "You two could be very useful to me. Come, sit down and let's talk."

When neither of you moves, he adds, "Please don't worry about your friend. He's quite safe, and so will you be. He just didn't suit my purposes, I'm afraid."

He sits down on a huge leather couch and beckons you to a set of leather chairs close by. You decide it's better to go along with the man until you can figure out what's going on. You walk over to the chair nearest Kainoa. Sonja follows. The whole time you still have a sense that your mind is being examined.

"What are you doing?" you ask.

"A bright kid; I like that," he answers. "I'm investigating certain components. What I find is quite interesting. So you have connections with Teledynamics?"

Choices: You pretend you don't know what he's talking about (turn to page 79).
You tell him about the contest and Dynamos (turn to page 84).

You fiddle with the computer keys for about fifteen minutes as the green snake continues its menacing dance on the screen. Nothing about a computer frightens you. You know that you have control of the situation.

Or do you?

You begin to itch all over and so you look down. Red welts and watery blisters are popping out all over your arms and hands. The places where you scratch begin to burn. You touch your face and feel the same phenomenon there. You've got them all over your body!

You run out of the room in search of Kikukawa. Neither she nor her companions are anywhere to be found. You run out the front door to look for the helicopter. It's still there, but you don't know what good it will do you. You can't sit down or hold onto anything without suffering. Every touch against your body sears like fire.

You scream out for Kikukawa, for anyone, to come relieve your misery. When you finally face the fact that you've been deserted, you try to calm down enough to figure out what to do.

Choices: You decide to try and work out a code that will stop the dancing snake (turn to page 81).
You run screaming through the canyon in hope someone will return to help you (turn to page 145).

The man with the jade rings points to a city below you. "Kaunakaki. We'll be stopping here a minute to get some things. Don't try anything funny. I've got lots of friends here."

The copter lands without a bump in a grassy field just outside town. The man shoves you out and grabs hold of your arm. You walk quickly down the center of town, past several businesses. A Japanese woman in a bakery window waves at you and then rushes out with two warm sweet rolls. Your captor takes one without a word. You take the other and smile at the woman.

You keep marching down the sidewalk with your arm gripped close to the man's. Then without warning he turns into the street, right in front of a galloping horse. He tumbles to the ground, and you feel yourself sliding across the pavement.

You feel the sharp sting of scrapes and bruises as you pick yourself up. You peer over at your companion. He's lying still on the street, the woman who had been riding the horse is bending over him.

Choices: You rush back toward the friendly Japanese woman in hope of getting help (turn to page 82).

You speed toward a nearby fish shop (turn to page 90).

Bert and Jade grumble about the foolishness of women as Kikukawa chases after Olawa. Seki and his father pace and circle the cave floor. The two servants slink back into a corner. Bert glances at his watch. "It's about time we got back to the house. It's been over an hour."

He hands you the lantern. "We've got a little business to take care of first. You go ahead with the lantern. We know this little hole like the back of our hands."

"What about the others?" you ask.

"Don't worry about them; they can take care of themselves."

Jade agrees. "That's for sure. Now, get going."

You return down the narrow tunnel, now empty of rock people. You've gone about a hundred feet when a terrible crashing shakes you from behind. After a few moments of uncertainty, you run back. The cave opening you just left is now filled with boulders, mud, and debris. A river of mud is moving your way.

You run and run out of the cave and into the canyon. The ground feels as though it will break open any moment. You see the helicopter and run in that direction.

Turn to page 87.

From that time on, he completely ignores you. Apparently he has no patience with pretending, or lying. He turns to Sonja instead. "Tell me, young lady, how much has Teledynamics offered you for your little toy?"

Sonja speaks up for the first time. You're troubled to see that she seems to be warming up to the man. "They haven't set any figures yet. We're expecting hundreds, even thousands, of dollars. We may be famous," she adds.

The man's eyes gleam with approval. "You, my daughter, will most certainly be rich and famous. But you will need to watch what partnerships you make." He stands up and holds out his hand. "Come with me. Let me show you what I mean."

You watch nervously as Kainoa leads Sonja into an adjoining room.

Choices: You run after them and insist that Kainoa take you along, too (turn to page 86).

You chance staying where you are so you can do some investigating (turn to page 96).

"Hey, are you really reading that Bible?" the startled nurse asks.

"Sure. I've been learning all kinds of exciting things. All about Saint Paul's beatings and stonings and shipwrecks and . . ."

"Well," she interrupts with a laugh, "that ought to make your wound seem less severe." Then she gets serious. "Say, we sure could use you down in Room 406."

"What do you mean?" you question.

"We've got a retarded eighteen-year-old down there scheduled for surgery in the morning. He's very scared about his strange surroundings and what's going to happen. His mother's been reading him the Bible for hours—it's the only thing that keeps him calm. We've been trying to find someone to relieve her, so she can go home and get some rest."

"I'd be glad to read to him," you hear yourself say.

Turn to page 94.

You rush back into the computer room and stand over the keys. "Please help me, Lord," you pray feverishly.

With much discomfort you press down the keys as you try several possible solutions. Then you stop. A mysterious formula keeps going over and over in your mind.

"That doesn't make sense," you tell yourself. But you decide that anything is worth a try. You type out the old, familiar words, a part of the Dynamos lock system."

```
1 For N = 7 to 77
2 Print N, SQR(N) - INT (SQR [N] )
3 Next N
4 End
```

In just seconds the snake begins to disappear as the math formulas zip across the screen.

Several moments later the welts and blisters begin to shrink. An hour later you feel as good as new. "Thank you, Lord," is all you know to say to the empty room.

You watch the empty screen and try to put this all together. Although you can't figure out the computer logistics of what just happened, you begin to wonder if God hadn't helped you fight some kind of evil force with his supernatural power.

Just then you hear the front door slam. You quickly type NEW and press RETURN.

Turn to page 88.

"Do you speak English?" you say to the woman, as you stand panting just inside the bakery door.

"Sure do. How can I help you?" she says politely. "Aren't you the one who was with Jade?"

Jade! You say to yourself. *That figures.* Out loud you say, "Yes, but he's been holding me by force. I know you're probably a friend of his, but I need to get back to Honolulu as quickly as I can. Will you help me?"

The woman puts her finger over her mouth. "Shhh," she says. "This way . . ." She bustles over to a door opening and pulls open the curtain that covers it. You hurry through.

"Now tell me, where's Jade? And what has happened to you?" she says, leading you down a narrow corridor to a back room.

You explain your situation as you both sit down in a small office. You're surprised to see the latest model of Teledynamics computer sitting on a desk. Then she fills in a few details.

"Jade is a strong-arm man for NO-GRO, a powerful grass-roots political group here on Molokai. They're trying to discourage outsiders from buying up local land and putting in resorts and things. They want to keep Molokai as it is. Most of us have supported them, but lately there's been some trouble."

Turn to page 93.

Turn to page 93.

"Yes, yes, I know all about that," Kainoa says with impatience. "But tell me about your lock code. That's what interests me."

"How could you know about that?" Sonja exclaims. "Only Mr. Isham and a few officials from Teledynamics know that it exists."

Kainoa beams with delight. "I know many things that are whispered behind locked doors," he says, waving his arm across the room with a flourish. As he does this, a door next to the kitchen flies open, and you gape at a room as huge as an auditorium.

All along one wall is the most massive computer system you've ever seen. In the middle of the room is a large dish satellite receiver. As the three of you enter in, you also notice a strange green phosphorescent column swarming with slithering green snakes.

"What do you do with all this?" you ask Kainoa.

"Oh, no. This is as far as we go until I know where you stand. My partnerships are only a select few," he tells you.

Turn to page 92.

Kainoa doesn't answer "yes" or "no." He continues to act as if you're not even there. So you just follow them into a beautiful red room. The floors, walls, and ceiling are all covered with plush scarlet carpet. There are about twenty white chairs surrounding a long oak conference table. The only thing on the table is a huge globe of the world. Kainoa opens some red velvet curtains to reveal a whole wall that's a sunken window, looking out onto a perfect geographical replica of all the Hawaiian Islands. It's like a map, yet somehow you seem to be looking at the real thing. The trees and mountains and buildings look authentic.

"My home," Kainoa announces simply. "Now, young lady, explain to me about the Dynamos project."

Sonja tells him everything about Dynamos, even about the lock system. You try to warn Sonja as she blabbers away. However, she's as oblivious to you as Kainoa.

"I want that lock program," Kainoa thunders. "I'll pay any price or award you any honor. And to prove I can do it, watch this. . . ."

On the table beside you are suddenly piled hundreds of bundles of hundred-dollar bills. "That just now came from the international Teledynamics headquarters bank!" Kainoa claims.

Turn to page 91.

The ground shakes and rumbles all around you. You open the door of the chopper, climb in, and frantically check over the sticks and levers, trying to remember the moves you watched Jade make earlier.

You start the engine and pull up on the straight stick. The machine lifts with a jerk! Up, up, up . . . panic! A steep cliff wall looms ahead. Up, up, up some more . . . you make it over!

Now you pitch the crooked stick to forward just as you glance back at a spewing mass of rock, fire, and smoke exploding from the volcano. You slam the stick as far as it'll go. Ash and debris shoot all around you. You stand straight up. It looks as though the tail of the helicopter is on fire!

Turn to page 97.

You open the door to the computer room and stare into the eyes of the white-haired man in the animal skin cape. "You not dead?" he asks.

"No, I'm fine," you answer. Then you add, "Where are the others?"

"They ran for the cave. They didn't want to get the sickness. I go tell them you okay." The barefoot man runs off.

You sit at the computer and try to absorb all that has happened to you. Just as you're in the middle of experimenting with another program, Kikukawa and the others walk in. The two servants, Olawa, Seki, and Seki's father begin to chant strange words and fall to their knees.

"What's wrong with them?" you ask Kikukawa.

"They think you're a god because the snake curse didn't affect you. They feel you have special powers," she tells you.

Choices: You think that's neat and keep working on the computer (turn to page 138).

You are horrified and demand that Kikukawa tell them to stop immediately (turn to page 122).

No one's in the shop, but you slip and slide on some water on the floor. Finally you make it to the back of the shop. In the dim light you smash into something slimy and smelly hanging from the ceiling. You see a door and rush out into an alley.

To your right, just beyond the city, you see a hill with a few trees and farms. Maybe if you head that way . . . You're not quite sure what you'll do when you get there, but you sure don't want to run into any of Jade's "friends" that he mentioned.

As the sun begins to set, you're halfway up the small mountain. You spy what looks like a large, flat boulder in the distance next to a tree. A nice place to rest a moment, you think. When you reach the spot, you feel the heaviness of the night shadows around you. Now what will you do?

The "boulder" you chose to lie down on feels very furry or feathery. Suddenly the whole thing begins to rise. It's too late to jump off; instead you grab on with all your might. You see the tree and mountain far below you and look closely at your strange transportation.

Turn to page 132.

"How did you do that?" Sonja cries.

Kainoa doesn't seem reluctant to explain. "My computer," he says.

"But where is it? I didn't see you working any controls." Sonja glances around the room.

Kainoa roars with laughter. Then he offers, "The one of you," for the first time acknowledging your presence, "who can tell me where my computer is can have all that money!"

Choices: You ask to talk to Sonja privately about your guesses (turn to page 95).

You don't want to miss out on such an opportunity; you make a guess of your own (turn to page 107).

"Would you like to play with my toy?" he offers, as he walks over to the computer. "I don't use it much anymore myself. No need for it now," he says with an odd smile.

His secretive, arrogant attitude begins to irritate you.

Choices: You decide you'll show him what you can do with a computer (turn to page 103).
You ignore the computer and keep pumping him with questions (turn to page 113).

The woman continues. "There have been threats against local citizens who don't whole-heartedly support NO-GRO. Also, some mysterious accidents have happened to investors who come here looking at property. Many of us have been concerned, and some have suspected Jade."

"But why is he with Kikukawa and that gang?" you ask.

"Kikukawa was hired by the government to interview the old-timers left from the ancient Polynesian and Maori peoples, and to excavate some primitive drawings found on a cave near her place. My guess is that Jade has been keeping a close eye on the project, to guard the interests of NO-GRO. As long as Kikukawa uses the information to protect the old ways of the islanders, no problem. But if it's to be used for commercial purposes—" The woman stops. "Someone's in the shop!" she says.

Turn to page 118.

The nurse pushes you in a wheelchair to Room 406.

"Just talk to him as you would a friend," the nurse advises you. "He wants the assurance of a kind voice. Ring the buzzer if he gives you any trouble. By the way, his name's Shawn," she says as she goes out of the room.

You read through half the Psalms, followed by a chapter each from John, Acts, and Revelation. Shawn, his six-foot frame relaxed on the bed, never takes his eyes off you. When you switch over to the stories of Daniel in the lions' den and David's fight with the giant, Goliath, he turns on his side with his eyes open wide. You stop to talk to him.

"How are you, Shawn?"

"Fine," he says. "You know Jesus?"

The question astonishes you. "Why, yes, I do," you say. You hesitate a moment before you add, "Do you, Shawn? Do you know Jesus?"

The boy flashes a broad grin. He pulls down the sheet and presses his palm against his chest. "Inhere. Jesus is in my heart. Read more."

Turn to page 150.

Kainoa actually leaves the room, leaving the two of you alone.

"Sonja!" you say as quietly as possible. "This room may be bugged." You mouth the next words to her. "This guy's crazy. Whatever you do, don't give him that lock system. Don't even think about it. He may be able to read minds."

Sonja watches your lips impatiently. Then she says, out loud, "You're just jealous because he pays so much attention to me. And don't think you can maneuver that money away from me. . . ."

"But, Sonja," you mouth, "that's stolen money!"

"Ha!" she says. "He didn't actually take it; it just appeared. That's not the same!"

"But what's he up to? Why is he here? Where did he get that power? What's he done with B. J.?" You get so excited with your questions, you almost talk out loud.

Sonja sets her mouth in a stubborn frown. You sigh, just as Kainoa enters the room.

Choices: You make a guess where the computer is (turn to page 107).

You refuse to play his game (turn to page 116).

As you rise from the chair, you manage to tip over the table lamp. You catch it before it crashes to the floor. With a sigh of relief, you attempt to replace it on the table when you notice a peculiar object underneath. There's a brilliant blue polished rock inset that looks like a button or buzzer.

You press it. Immediately the living room is transformed into an office. There's a desk, and Mr. Isham is sitting behind it. You say "Hi," but he doesn't seem to notice you. He's talking to several committee members you recognize. You walk over right in front of him and wave your hand before his eyes. None of the men gives you the least attention.

You return to the lamp and press the rock again. This time the room changes to a rustic house with a group of interesting-looking people. You're shocked to see Dan and the other guide, Kikukawa. There's also a man wearing jade jewelry, a weird old man with an animal skin coat, and an old woman who's doing all the talking. You try to get their attention. Again, no one sees you.

Turn to page 142.

You know you're going to have to land quickly. You see only two fairly open, flat areas beneath you. To your far left is a lush valley of low-growing vegetation. About a dozen dwellings indicate a village.

To your far right you can see one lone house hugging the north coast. A neat garden and large meadow stretch out behind.

Choices: You head for the village (turn to page 101).

You dive down toward the meadow (turn to page 104).

"A blue whale!" one of the men informs you as he speeds by. You see the captain peering through binoculars at a tall, thick spout of water in the distance.

"Must be close to ninety feet long," he reports. "Probably wounded and gone crazy. Here it comes again! Shoot to kill!"

A volley of shots rings out. The next thing you know, the boat rises high beside an enormous hulk. The craft splits like a toothpick. You tumble down into tons of salty water. Your body heaves up and down several times before you gasp a breath of fresh air. Men holler all around you. You can also hear a faint yip. Hunks of floating debris surround you. You grab for one of them and look around frantically for Pilikia.

You spot him! He's shaking in fear as he clutches the back of the dying blue whale!

Choices: You chance getting close to the whale to try to rescue Pilikia (turn to page 102).
You call to the pup to jump off as you paddle toward shore (turn to page 130).

As you slowly canvass the room with care, you feel Kainoa's probe on your mind stronger than ever. This time it appears that he's not just circling around it, he's trying to enter inside. You want to fight him off, but your eagerness in finding the hidden computer is too strong.

Suddenly a clear voice commands, "Kiss the master's hand and you'll know all."

A terrible fight goes on in your head. You fear you'll split apart. All you have to do is kiss Kainoa's hand. No big deal. Except that it takes every ounce of power within you to keep from doing it.

In desperation you race out of the room screaming, "Lord Jesus, help me!"

Not only is your mind at peace again, but your overwhelming desire for the pile of money has gone. That's when you remember Sonja. You begin to pray earnestly for her, until she and Kainoa come back to the living room where you are.

You tremble in anticipation of Kainoa's response, but he surprises you. He saunters to the couch, plops down on it, and falls fast asleep.

Turn to page 125.

As you near your target, you see a crowd gathered just beyond the dwellings. They must have heard you coming or seen the trail of smoke.

How nice, you think, *a welcoming party.*

As you make your crash landing, you slide within yards of the group of people. You jump out as soon as the machine halts. That's when you realize what you've bumped yourself into.

A handful of families surround a woman in a white dress and veil, who holds the hand of a man in white shirt and pants. A man with a high collar, complete with lei, stands before them holding a Bible.

You've just interrupted a village wedding!

"Well," you say to yourself, "at least they'll have something to tell their children about this day."

THE END

As quietly as you can, you push closer and closer to the mammoth animal. You now understand with shocking force why this creature is called the largest animal that has ever lived on earth. You know these hundred-plus tons of blubber, even in the whale's weakened state, could kill you with a single swish of that tail.

Or what if it swallowed me alive like Jonah? you wonder with horror.

What gives you some courage is the fact that Pilikia's clawing and yelping hasn't stirred the whale from its stationary position. As you edge closer, you cringe as you realize you're swimming in a pool of blood.

Suddenly, the whale stirs. . . .

Choices: You grab the nearest thing to you—the whale's fin (turn to page 106).
You shove yourself away from the whale as fast as you can (turn to page 130).

"Very good," Kainoa confesses as he watches you for over an hour.

"This certainly has more than 64K Memory, doesn't it?" you finally ask.

"My young friend," Kainoa answers, "this computer has been built to receive as much memory as the full capacity of the human brain." He pauses. "You do know, of course, that we Homo sapiens use but a tiny percentage of our total brain capacity?"

You nod.

"Well, my computer friend and I have eliminated that problem. I happen to be gifted with a photographic memory. I've been exercising my mind for years now to retain more and more. Whatever is in that computer's core is also in my mind right now."

"But, how . . . ?"

"Don't worry about it. You could never understand. I am unlike any man who has ever lived. Olawa the Great will be very proud of me. I am in contact with her even now. . . ."

A loud buzzing interrupts his talk.

Turn to page 108.

The meadow is farther than you first antici-
pated. By the time you try to land, smoke cuts
off most of your vision. You crash into something. *I sure hope it's not the house,* you think to
yourself as you tumble forward.

Soon a woman and a gang of children bend
over you. You're on the ground and the helicopter is smoldering next to a smashed-in grass hut.
"The chicken house," the woman tells you.

After they see that you're all right, they rush
to rescue their chickens and put out the fire in
the copter.

"We're the Kekahuna family," the woman says cheerfully. "It's not often we get company. You're welcome to stay as long as you want— and that may be some time. Your copter has suffered some major damage. Some of the rotors burned, too."

She introduces you to a pair of twins. "These are Robert and Lisa, two of my eight children. We're marooned here right now, since we lost our boats in the last storm. But we'll get you home sooner or later."

Turn to page 109.

You hold on as tightly as you can to the slippery fin. Your sore arm feels numb. Water begins to spray over you as the enormous fish picks up speed. You can't see a thing. But then, just as abruptly as he took off, the whale slows down and sinks a bit.

You notice that you're close to shore. The whale appears to be grounded. You stand up in the shoulder-deep water and shout to Pilikia to jump down. The puppy takes a flying leap and misses your outstretched arm. He sputters around in the foam, and then paddles furiously towards land.

You glance back to see the broad tail swinging in your direction.

Turn to page 110.

You have a brilliant flash. "It's a tiny remote in your pocket!" you announce with pride.

"Nice guess," Kainoa says, emptying out his purple pockets. "However, as you can see . . . "

"I know, I know!" Sonja says as she jumps and claps. "It's in your head! The computer is your own brain!"

Kainoa looks at her with obvious pleasure. "Good, you have passed the first test. A good transfer," he says in a way that makes your skin crawl.

You know you're up against something you've never known before. It frightens you. Kainoa has some supernatural aura about him. But, is it from God? If it isn't . . . The alternatives make you feel very uneasy.

Kainoa walks over to the window looking out on the Islands. "Come here, Sonja, my dear," he says, "I will give you the second test."

Choices: You push Kainoa through the window from behind (turn to page 111).
You sneak out the door while they're not noticing you (turn to page 114).

While you and Kainoa have been talking, Sonja has been sauntering around the room, inspecting this and that. She apparently pulled a lever next to a beeping red light that activated a propelling force. You now see her rising up through the ceiling as the whole mountain roof expands wide open. You see a brilliant display of sky and stars above you.

Kainoa raises his hand toward Sonja.

Choices: You jump on Kainoa to try and buy Sonja a little more time (turn to page 124).

You rush over to the lever that Sonja pulled and push it harder (turn to page 141).

After you've rested and eaten and had the nasty cut on your forehead bandaged by Mrs. Kekahuna, Robert and Lisa tell you about their life here in the wilderness.

"Our mother teaches us everything. We have school six days a week. And we take care of the garden and tend the animals," Lisa explains.

"And I'm a fisherman," Robert adds. "Come on! We'll show you around. I'll bring my spear along, just in case. . . ."

"Just in case what?" you ask with some apprehension.

"Oh, I might see a squid or a wild pig. We've got to hunt our own meat, you know," he says nonchalantly.

Turn to page 137.

The next thing you know, the heat of the sun's rays beats down on your back. A female voice breaks through your semiconsciousness. Gentle hands turn you over. "Carry the child to my cottage," the pleasant voice orders. "The dog, too."

You squint your eyes open enough to catch sight of a woman's face tightly wrapped around with white cloths. "An angel," you murmur. "I must be in heaven."

Turn to page 112.

Kainoa crashes through the glass and you stare as you see him in the Hawaiian landscape. He's small and on a shore of a Lanai beach.

You grab at Sonja. "Let's get out of here!" you shout.

But she yanks away from you. "No! I want to go with Kainoa!" she says, and jumps through the window.

Choices: You jump in after her (turn to page 147).
You try to get out of this underground house and find help (turn to page 128).

Later you wake up in a small, dimly lighted room. "I'm glad to see you're better," the white-draped "angel" says. "I'm Sister Maria. You are in Kalaupapa. The dog that washed up with you is fine, though he swallowed much water, too. In fact, one of our residents, Ponciano, has taken him for a walk."

"Is there any way out of this place, so I can get back to Honolulu?" you ask as you suddenly remember the demonstration.

"Oh, yes," she assures you. "You can travel by mule train with the tourists up the mountain in the morning. Someone at the park should be able to direct you to some transportation from there. Or you could wait for the plane. I can't guarantee just when the flight will be in—maybe this week, maybe next. The schedule for the leper colony here isn't very regular."

"Leper colony!" you repeat. Your skin starts to have a crawly feeling as you shrink back on the cot.

"Oh, please don't worry," she hurries to tell you. "The patients aren't contagious. Modern medicines have worked miracles."

Choices: You take your chances with the mule ride, just so you get out of there quickly (turn to page 129).
You decide to wait for the plane. You don't feel up to a ride on a mule (turn to page 115).

"How did you get this stuff down here? Why do you keep so hidden?" you demand.

"QUIET!" Kainoa roars. "You don't amuse me anymore. I haven't time to orient you. I'll have to dispose of you."

He looks over at the column of snakes and stares in a trancelike state. One of the snakes slides off and slithers toward you. You try to escape. Then everything goes black.

THE END

You try to find someplace to hide while you think through what your next possible action could be. The living room has no cubbyholes that you can see.

You press along the wall into the kitchen. Just off the kitchen is a closed door. You try the handle. Locked. You check through the kitchen cupboards and find a bin that rolls forward. There are some coconuts in there, but there's enough room for you. You crawl in and lean back. The bin closes.

Turn to page 151.

You decide to take a walk around the leper colony. The disfigured bodies of the residents shock you at first, but everyone seems friendly. They wave at you with mangled stubs where their hands should be. You figure the least you can do is wave back with your healthy limbs.

You stop for a while at a booth where a man sits at a table working on a craft project. You marvel at the way he manages to use his tools. When the man looks up at you, you gape at his misshapen nose. "Smile!" he tells you. "It no break your face!"

You laugh uncertainly and ask him what he's doing.

"Make jewelry," he says, and points to a dolphin-shaped object. "Make from sandbox tree seeds. You like?"

You nod and study with amazement the unusual, polished stonelike material. Just then Sister Maria walks up. "I see you've met Ponciano. He's quite a help to me here in the colony."

Ponciano bows his head slightly in embarrassment. You're surprised to notice how quickly his handicaps fade into the background as his personality comes through.

"Come," Sister Maria beckons to you. "I want to show you something."

Turn to page 117.

Kainoa flies into a rage. "I am Kainoa!" he reminds you. "Don't trifle with me!"

Then, just as suddenly as he became enraged, he calms right down and continues the game with Sonja. A plan forms in your mind. You know your thoughts are private as long as he's busy with Sonja. You set things up. Then your plan goes into operation.

Turn to page 152.

She takes you to the beach where a dozen or so lepers are cutting away at the whale.

"We'll use the blubber for oil," Sister Maria explains. "We'll use some of the meat for eating and the rest for fertilizer. Quite a bonanza for us."

For the next week you attend movies at the local theater, learn from Ponciano how to make dolphin jewelry for the tourists, and play with Pilikia. Then, about noon one day, you hear the roar of a small jet. You and Pilikia run out to the airfield to watch the landing.

That afternoon the pilot takes you on a search to look for the captain and his crew. You spot them down the coast on a small inlet. You throw down some sacks of provisions that Sister Maria had wrapped for you. One or two of them land on the tiny shore. The third splashes into the ocean nearby. That's the one containing your note, saying that help will be coming soon—just as soon as you reach Honolulu.

THE END

The woman returns to report, "Jade's in the hospital with a possible concussion. You're safe for the time being. That was Mrs. Naki, the woman who ran you down. She's offered to give you a ride to the airport." She pulls a purse out of a desk drawer. "Here, this money will get you to Honolulu. God bless you."

"God bless you, too, and thank you!" you say. "I'll get the money paid back as soon as I get to my luggage."

"Please don't worry about it. Your story has helped confirm that Jade's a man who must be watched. He has too much power here to ever convict him, without some public outcry first. However, there are ways."

You suddenly believe this woman could do just about anything she sets out to do. There's something about the set of her jaw and the look in her eye. . . . For a brief second, you feel sorry for Jade.

You meet Mrs. Naki out in the front of the shop. The Japanese woman hands you a bag of pastries and helps you up on the black horse that has a yellow-and-orange lei around its neck.

THE END

The man with the glazed eyes accelerates onto the highway. You clutch the back of a seat and sit down. Seven others are crammed into the vehicle: four guys and three girls. One of them pulls you out of your seat and plunks you down on a lap. "Well, ain't you cute?" says a dreamy voice.

Without warning, you tumble and toss on top of the other passengers. The van seems to be rolling. You collide into heads, bodies, and sharp objects. You collapse in a heap.

The next sounds you hear are moans and the metallic buzz of a machine. You can't move without sharp pain, so you just keep still. Maybe this is all a dream; you hope you'll wake up soon.

You feel arms pulling you. You cry out.

"Don't worry, kid," someone says. "You'll be all right. Took us some time to cut you out."

You're placed on a stretcher and pushed into an ambulance. "Book them all," you hear an officer say. "There's enough dope in there to hold them all without bond . . . the ones that survived, that is."

THE END

You and Kikukawa find Myra and the others out on the beach. They had just decided to change clothes and spend some time at the miniature golf course which Myra said features waterfalls, volcanoes, and fancy pagoda buildings.

As you walk back to the hotel to carry in your luggage and micro, you pull Kikukawa aside. "But what about those men you were with? Won't they come after us?"

"Bert will understand, but I'm not sure about Jade. He was the one with the rifle. He's always made me feel a little uneasy. That's why I didn't tell the guys what I was doing. But I've got a friend I can call who'll keep an eye out for us. He's a bodyguard for a wealthy *haole,* that is, a mainlander. He's on vacation this week."

Kikukawa calls her bodyguard friend, and he checks out the meadow where the helicopter landed. He reports back that Bert, Jade, and the helicopter are gone. You don't hear any more about them until the morning you, Sonja, and Dan climb up the jet steps to return to the States. There in the crowd, behind Myra and Kikukawa, stands Jade!

You wonder all the way home what happened next.

THE END

You're trying to think how you can either gracefully get out of this or psych yourself into sliding down that waterfall. Robert and Lisa have jumped out of the pool and are gazing expectantly at you.

Just at that moment you see something ferocious looking bearing down on them from behind. "Look out!" you shriek.

Robert turns and spears the boar with lightning speed, right between the eyes. The wild pig flails to the earth and soon lies still. You watch from your perch as Robert and Lisa fashion a tough hammock from branches and foliage around them. They carry their prize back up the hill. You offer to help. "No thanks," says Lisa. "It's a two-man job."

As you hike back to the Kekahuna home, you marvel at the strength and ability of these backwoods kids. Your horror of the volcanic eruption and anxiety about returning to Honolulu eases somewhat in these peaceful, frontier surroundings.

"There's a lot a computer whiz kid like me can learn from people like this," you say to yourself, and settle down for a possible long-term stay.

THE END

You explain to them all as simply as you can. "I'm a Christian. The Christ I serve was sent to heaven by God, his Father, to defeat the works of evil on this earth. I called upon Christ to help me and he did. That's why I was able to be healed of the curse's disease on my body."

You tell them that no human being should be worshiped as a god. Olawa bows low just one more time and leaves the room. Soon the others follow after her. You work in peaceful silence for at least half an hour, deciphering the lock. You're amazed at how quickly the whole thing falls into place.

Bert and Jade come in at one point and ask Kikukawa if they can go into Kaunakaki with the helicopter. She tells them to get a report on the volcano from Olawa.

"I did it!" you shout. "It's working again."

Just at that moment Olawa runs in with news. "Volcano will erupt soon. We must go. Bert and Jade, take the child and that," she points to the computer, "in the helicopter. The rest of us still have time to make it out of the pass."

You scurry around grabbing the equipment and race to the copter. You squeeze everything in and zoom into the air. "I'll come right back for the others, as soon as we reach Kaunakaki," Bert assures you.

THE END

The game you're playing reminds you of hockey. You see the other riders hitting a ball with their sticks, aiming at a goalpost. Sometimes the players change horses. You keep expecting someone to say, "Hey, you, what are you doing here?" But the game keeps going.

In the last minute of the last period, several opponents charge at you full tilt as you lash the ball across the line. Your team wins, but you wind up on the ground with the whip curled around you.

Back in the gym, several of the players clap you on the back. "Good playing, Hitchcock. We thought you'd be out of it as usual, but you came through. You're still the best polo player in the lot."

You smile, turn in your uniform and equipment to the locker marked "Hitchcock," and try again to find Myra and Sonja.

THE END

Kainoa is amazingly lightweight for all the power his physical presence exudes. You knock him down easily, and he whimpers like a baby. "You've sprained my hand," he cries. "Now look what you've done." Then he actually sobs.

You run over to the lever by the red beeping light and push it down hard. You fly up quickly and the ceiling opens wider. The freedom of flight and, of course, escape feels good. But as you ascend, you wonder how and where you'll land.

As you rise closer to the stars, you realize that those lights aren't stars after all. They're millions of fireflies surrounding you. Off in the distance you see an amazing sight—at least a dozen hot-air balloons sailing in the bright moonlight. If only you could get close enough to grab on to one.

But it's no use. You begin to descend. It's a slow, pleasant ride down. It occurs to you that if Kainoa ever used this mode of transportation, he surely would have it set for a soft landing.

It is. You float comfortably down to the top of a large palm tree near town. Now all you have to do is slide down the trunk.

THE END

"We've got to get out of here," Sonja says. "Fast!" You both search for an outside door or other exit. Sonja finds a locked door by the kitchen. "I can pick that lock easy," she says, as she rummages through the kitchen doors. She finds a single table knife.

She pries the door open. You both gasp at what you see inside. A huge computer lines one entire wall. An enormous dish satellite receiver stands in the middle. On one side a glowing column of fat, slithery green snakes crawl up and down. But that's not all. The wall across from you contains a living panorama of the city of Honolulu.

"Look, there's our hotel," Sonja shows you. "It looks as though we could walk right over to it."

"What about the snakes?" you remind her, as one slides down from the column.

"Let's make a run for it," she challenges. In seconds you're standing in front of your hotel. Sonja looks behind you and shrieks. A snake is coiled in the street.

As you watch, transfixed, a tour bus runs over it. You continue to stare as the remains completely disintegrate. No trace is left of your underground adventure.

THE END

Wednesday night you, Dan, and Sonja present your Dynamos game to the international representatives of Teledynamics. They applaud your intricate graphics. Many take turns playing the game and make comments like, "Never had such an exciting run before!" Even their top expert claims, "Challenging plays!"

Mr. Isham, the president, challenges each of them to try and break into the lock system. No one can.

Later, after a dinner of steak tartare and lime pie, you sign the contract. Just as you hand the pen to Mr. Isham, you look straight into the eyes of a smirking face: Sammy!

The president places his arm around the boy's shoulders. "Have I introduced you to my son?"

THE END

The nurse takes your temperature and blood pressure; then she hands you some pills and a glass of water.

After you wash the pills down, the nurse makes a quick turn, flips out the light, and softly closes the door.

THE END

You look throughout the house. It has a kitchen, a bathroom, a bedroom, the living room, and a room that's locked. There are no outside doors. No way out and no way in except by Kainoa's mysterious traveling-through-mountain-walls trick.

There's some food in the cupboard, so you eat some crackers and cheese. You drink some papaya and coconut juice out of the refrigerator. That's when you notice something else strange. There are no plug outlets anywhere in the house. All the appliances and lights have some other kind of energy source.

You return to the red room. The window is still broken, but the Hawaiian Islands have vanished. There's just a wall of dirt there.

You return to the kitchen to look for some kind of digging tool. You're surprised to see that the food you ate has been replaced. The bottle of juice is full again. The crackers and cheese are the same as before you sampled them. You find one single table knife. "Kainoa must not have to bother with such things as utensils," you muse to yourself. "Probably lasers his food instead."

You try to dig through the dirt wall behind the window. You're no dummy. You know you're going to be there a long time.

THE END

Very early the next morning Sister Maria introduces you to the mule-train guide, a man named Quincy. She helps you slide up on your animal, ties down a sack of food for you, and waves good-bye as Pilikia runs besides you.

The trail is much steeper in places than you imagined. You keep your eyes straight ahead on Quincy's back so you won't panic. You figure anything's better than staying in Kalaupapa. But you also have lots of time to think. An uncomfortable thought stabs you: Didn't Jesus spend a lot of time with lepers? Even touch them?

Several hours later you reach a sort of ranger station. Quincy tells an official-looking person that you need to get to Honolulu.

"You're in luck," the man tells you. "Our helicopter leaves in half an hour for Oahu."

Before you know it, you and Pilikia are flying high over Molokai. It isn't until you coast down into the Honolulu heliport that you remember the captain and crew. Your stomach churns as you wonder what happened to them.

THE END

You watch from the safety of your wood plank as the whale scoots towards shore with Pilikia bawling from on top. You hear the captain and the other men calling to the pup to jump. None of them ventures near the whale.

You continue to float with the current downstream. Soon, the whale and his rider are out of sight as you turn a slight bend. Down the coast you travel for several miles. Finally, you see a small inlet with some tree branches sticking out that you can grab. You pull yourself onto shore and look back to see the other crewmen doing the same. The captain takes roll. "Only one man unaccounted for . . . and Pilikia," he announces.

"What do we do now?" you ask, as you stare in awe at the sheer cliffs hundred of feet high surrounding you.

"We'll have to wait for a boat or plane to spot us. That could be days . . . or weeks. Meanwhile, we'd better see what kind of gear we've got."

One of the men carried a sack of candy bars. Another had tied a bag of nuts around his waist. You find several packs of waterproof containers with matches. "And we'll do a little fishing," the captain encourages you all. "Before you know it, we'll be back to civilization."

"I'd settle for being dry," you murmur as you shiver in the cool evening breeze.

THE END

You find yourself flying behind Manu on his motorcycle. There is dust in your eyes, in your nose, in your mouth, everywhere. You fight to keep the tears back as your arm bounces around.

After an endless battle with pelting dirt, Manu screeches to a halt outside what looks like a ranch headquarters. You hope that somewhere near are a bathtub and bed that you can use. Manu leads you inside where a fair-skinned man with red hair is scurrying around.

"Are you the doctor?" you ask hopefully.

"Nahh. Used to be a medic in the war, though . . . sort of. The doc's out riding bulls."

Manu asks him to look at your arm. "Yep, broken, all right. Right smack down the middle. I'll take care of you soon as I get back. Looking for my gear for the calf-roping contest. Got a good chance of beating out the doc for 'All Around.' Come to think of it, he may want to look at that himself. Make yourself comfy."

The red-haired man disappears down the road. Manu takes you to a cot in an adjoining room. He asks if you're hungry. You don't answer. You feel your eyelids closing, and the last thing you hear are whoops and hollers and an announcer saying, "And here comes Red Rider out of the gate. . . ."

THE END

It's a bird of some kind—a lot like a vulture, only much larger. It has a long hooked beak that extends almost straight out from a flat forehead. Its head is bald and yellow, its neck reddish in the moonlight. Its wings are at least ten feet wide. You feel as though you've landed in a Mother Goose story or something. "Well," you say to yourself, "if only I can hang on, this thing's got to land sometime."

However, the bird flies on and on all night and all the next day. You have some real scares when it swoops down to pick up some small animals that washed up on some tiny islands in the ocean and devours them in midair.

Either two or three days later the huge fowl comes down to earth . . . sort of. She lands on top of a high, craggy cliff, where she proceeds to build a nest and lays two white eggs.

You have no idea where you are. You figure it's possible you're somewhere in South America, by the direction you've been traveling. The cliffs all around you resemble pictures you've seen of the Andes Mountains.

On the third day, you notice a spiral of smoke coming from down the mountain. There must be a village down there. Gingerly you begin your descent in that direction.

THE END

At last a policeman picks you up. You detail what happened, and he returns you to the hotel. "I've put in a report to the local force and the Molokai force. We should have no trouble rounding them up soon. We'll get back to you tomorrow about whether you'll want to press charges."

You introduce the officer to Myra, Sonja, and Dan. "Say," he says, "how would you kids like some mopeds to ride while you're on the island?"

You look at each other. "We've got four we picked up last week," he continues. "You're welcome to use them for a couple days."

You all let out a whoop as Myra gives her permission. You're soon riding in style along the beachside roads, out to see the famous Diamond Head, an extinct volcano.

THE END

You corner Sonja in the hotel restaurant game room. She plays a perfect round of Centipede while you explain all you know about Kikukawa's strange actions.

"But that's a criminal act!" Sonja protests. "You could have been killed, or—or missed the demonstration!"

"Which would have been worse?" you tease.

"We've got to tell Myra!" Sonja insists, ignoring your question. "This Kikukawa may be a very dangerous person. Maybe she's an escaped prisoner or something."

"Wait a minute—she did bring me back," you remind her.

"Oh, sure. But maybe she decided Dan or I would be a better prospect. What if she's just waiting for a chance to grab us? Then how would your conscience feel?"

You admit that the thought hadn't crossed your mind.

"So that settles it," Sonja says, knocking out another centipede.

The next day the Honolulu papers carry the headlines: "LOCAL KIDNAPPING BY MOLOKAI TERRORISTS," with your picture on the front page.

Mr. Isham commends you. "Good publicity for Teledynamics."

THE END

Bert, Jade, and the others stay where they are, as they yell at you and Kikukawa to come back. You can't throw off the appeal of that siren noise. It seems to compel you to keep going.

Then a low rumble and roar gradually drown out the high tone. Kikukawa says at last, "The creatures are going home and they're taking Olawa with them. We can't go any farther."

You stop before a steamy, dark lake that scalds your finger when you touch it. You watch as the rock people roll into it and disappear. As the last creature falls into the boiling brine, Olawa steps off into the lake. She never cries out or says a word as she sinks quickly into its depths.

"Why did she do that?" you ask. "Why didn't you try to stop her?"

"What difference does it make now?" she said. "The volcano has begun to erupt, and we're on the inside."

THE END

You go barefoot, because Robert and Lisa do. But you carry your shoes along in a knapsack that's also filled with dried bananas, dried fish, and dried figs.

You walk along a trail that leads to a wooded area and ask Lisa about the scraggly looking trees.

"Kukui trees," she explains. "We use the nuts for lamp oil." Then she points excitedly. "There's Lei Lani. Last one down is a barracuda."

You and Robert chase after Lisa as she runs up the hill you're on. You stop at the edge— you're right next to a thirty-foot waterfall that plunges into a pinkish pool.

Lisa sits right on top without hesitation and slides down with a delighted cheer. Robert automatically starts to do the same; then he turns back to you. "Will you be all right?"

You say "sure" with more boldness than you feel. Robert throws his spear down the falls first, and then slips like a seal down into the pool.

Turn to page 121.

For over an hour the little band of chanters continue their religious rite of some kind. You're beginning to find it hard to think or even concentrate as you continue to work through various computer programs for unlocking the hexed machine.

You feel yourself growing irritated and frustrated. You turn around and yell, "Shut up!" to the group. They just chant all the louder. You run out of the room to find Kikukawa. "Can't you get these people to be quiet so I can work in peace?" you ask her.

"They feel you're the answer to their deliverance from the curse. They're afraid if they stop, your god will be angry with them."

"But that's ridiculous! Meanwhile, my mind's so muddled I can't even remember the simplest BASIC." You stop as the ground rumbles beneath you. "What's that?"

"The volcano. Olawa hasn't been keeping track of its moods." Kikukawa rushes out the door. You run after her.

The two of you watch in awe as thick black and gray clouds spew out of the top. "We're too late!" Kikukawa gasps. "We'll never make it out of this canyon. And Bert and Jade have the helicopter down at Kaunakaki getting provisions."

The air sizzles with fumes and you all cough for air.

THE END

Soon you find Myra and Sonja out on the beach, headed to a luau. A log drum beats for the dancers, and a rhythmic game called *tititorea* is being organized for the tourists.

Sonja tells you they're going to serve things like crab fingers, Mahi Mahi, and Opakapaka, a kind of seafood. You don't care if it does sound weird. You're hungry enough to eat anything.

You dig right into a huge appetizer plate piled with bananas, lichees, and mandarin oranges.

THE END

You roll out of the way of the horses' hooves and bound back to the gym. You hear yells from behind of "Hitchcock! Get back here!"

You fling off the hat and uniform as fast as you can and sprint to the door. No use. The same native tackles you again and you crash to the floor.

A couple players rush in and shout a few words in Hawaiian to the native. Then they say to each other, "A few days of drying out in the tank will teach Hitchcock a thing or two."

The next thing you know, you're behind bars. You tell the guard over and over, "I'm not Hitchcock. I'm a kid who won a contest and I'm supposed to be at the hotel and . . ."

Finally they allow you a phone call to Myra.

THE END

Immediately you shoot up through the mountain opening right behind Sonja. As you rise above the treetops you feel a slight slowing down of your speed, like a tug pulling you back.

At that moment you pass and barely miss an object floating in the sky. You look around you. In the bright moonlight you recognize hordes of hot-air balloons. You cry out to Sonja, "Grab one of those balloons!"

Arms stretch out of the one nearest you and yank you in. "Amazing what you'll fish out of the sky these days," someone says.

"Yessir," says another. "Hope it's edible; I'm starving."

Sonja is safe in a nearby balloon. You learn that you've run into an expedition of balloonists who are crossing the Pacific Ocean. They are most unwilling to allow you to land. "We've got to remain aloft or we lose the race, matey," they explain. "Next stop: Japan, or thereabouts."

THE END

You press the stone one more time. The scene in the room changes once more to an office—a very impressive office. The United States seal and flag are there. The President sits behind the desk. The Secretary of State and an important-looking dignitary sit before him.

You immediately press the stone again. The room returns to its former state. You shudder as the implications of what you've just seen sink in.

You determine at that moment that somehow you and Sonja are going to flee from here. Somehow you're going to relay what you've just witnessed to the right people. And somehow you'll get them to listen.

You set your face in a pleasant smile and walk nonchalantly into the room that Kainoa and Sonja just entered.

THE END

The next thing you know you're in your hotel-room bed. You seem to be waking from some kind of bad dream, but you can't even remember what it was about. After a moment, you crawl under the covers and go to sleep.

The next morning, you're startled to see that you've slept all night in your clothes and shoes. Myra knocks at your door all excited because Sonja can't be found. After a search of the hotel and the beach, Myra calls her friend, B. J. He helps you look, too. One of the dining-room waiters tells you he thought he saw her leave last night with a couple men. But he didn't get a good look at them.

Myra reports her missing to the police. Late that evening a patrol car finds her wandering along the highway that leads to the rain forest. She can't remember how she got there or anything about the last twenty-four hours.

But after a nice hot shower and a tasty meal, she's back to her old self. You and Sonja spend the rest of your Honolulu trip listening to some wild tales that Dan spouts about his adventures on the way to Waikiki.

THE END

"The best defense is never to think about such things," you admonish. "The Bible tells us to keep our thoughts on good things, pure things . . . stuff like that. Which reminds me, Myra, when do we eat?"

THE END

Someone runs out of a cave carrying a big, heavy army blanket and throws it over you. You scream in agony as the scratchy material rubs against your blistery skin.

The person picks you up and runs with you. You can't see a thing, because the blanket is over your head, too. The next thing you know, you're lifted up into the seat of the helicopter and the blanket pulled down from your head.

"Take this off me!" you yell.

Bert answers, "I'm sorry, but I can't. You're highly contagious. I'm going to get you to Kaunakaki as quick as I can. That's the only chance you've got."

You almost pass out from pain every time you move or the helicopter hits an air pocket. Bert lands right in the doctor's backyard and tries to gently carry you into the house. You're unconscious for most of the next couple weeks. When you come to, the doctor tells you that Bert is busy at Kikukawa's place . . . trying to dig it out. There was a volcanic eruption there and it's assumed that no one survived.

THE END

Mr. Isham of Teledynamics commends you for your honesty and announces that the international committee still wants the patent to Dynamos. They're prepared to pay each of you $50,000 or $2,000 per year for life, whichever you prefer. They may still want the lock system, anyway.

You give your presentation of the game on Wednesday night. The Teledynamics representatives respond with enthusiasm. There's also a big surprise—Sammy is there, too. He turns out to be Mr. Isham's son!

You, Sonja, Dan, and Sammy spend hours together that night developing a variation on the original lock. You eventually develop a system that even Sammy couldn't get into.

THE END

You're sure this isn't the same beach that Kainoa landed on. The cliff line and curve of the shore is different. You search around to see if Sonja may have come here. After hours of looking and calling her name, you realize you're a million miles from nowhere. No signs of civilization. Not even any wildlife. Sheer cliffs jut out all along the coast. Not being a rock climber, you see no hope of escaping in that direction.

As it gets dark, you huddle against the cliffs to get some warmth. All night you listen to the wind and dig down into the sand. The stark aloneness you feel brings you close to sheer terror.

You remember to pray, and feel immediate comfort. You realize for the first time how Jonah must have felt in the middle of that fish.

The next morning, you see the sails of a boat out on the ocean's horizon. You jump and wave your hands as hard as you can. Eventually, the boat docks near you. A young woman hops out of the dinghy. "Is this Maui?" she asks. "I'm in a sailing heat from San Francisco. I want to report my time."

You tell her you're more lost than she is. She gives you a ride as you search for a familiar beach.

THE END

The next thing you know, Sonja is beside you exclaiming over some plants and vegetation that you've fallen into. A translucent brightness shines on and through the foliage.

"Look," Sonja points, "we must be behind the waterfall. It's some kind of underground garden."

You can feel the spray where you are. Now the smells hit you. Ginger, clove, jasmine . . . You reach up and pull some large, smooth, shiny seeds off a tree. The nut inside has an oily, sweet flavor. *How can these things grow here underground?* you marvel to yourself.

You feel very lazy. You can't seem to remember where you are. You look over at Sonja. She's lying down in a grassy place and yawning. You think you see a man sitting beside a pool nearby watching you both. You sit up to greet him, but your eyes are so heavy. All you can think of is sleep . . . sleep . . . sleep.

THE END

The time passes quickly. Before you know it, Shawn's mother returns. She thanks you repeatedly and offers to pay you. You refuse the money and tell her you'd be glad to come back anytime.

As the nurse wheels you back to your room, she tells you, "In the morning you can read to Mr. Samuelson. He's only got a few days left, but he's alert enough to hear what's going on. And then there's a woman in intensive care. We think she might come around if someone spent some time talking to her. She has no family around."

You feel a happy sense of satisfaction as you share with others the holy book you had almost been ashamed of.

THE END

You feel air on your back. You reach behind you in the blackness into open space. You back up and stretch your hands all around.

The opening isn't huge—about three feet wide. You twist around and try to crawl. The surface feels muddy, cool, and firm. As you creep you begin to ascend. Then, you bump into something smooth and hard, like pipes. You climb up and over the pipes and pull yourself onto a flat dirt surface. You fall against some stacked barrels. They smell like rotten grapes.

You can see a stairway ahead of you, so you walk over and climb up. Creak, creak, creak . . . As soon as you swing the door wide, you understand where you are: inside the haunted mansion.

At every step through the house, out the front, and down to the forest road, you half expect to be sucked back. But you make it to B. J.'s car, which is right where he left it. There are even some keys. You drive it back to the hotel and wake everyone. What a surprise to find Sonja there with Myra. A quick call to B. J.'s apartment rouses him. Neither Sonja or B. J. admit they know anything of what you're talking about.

THE END

152

You draw Kainoa's attention to yourself by unwinding the money bundles as he teases Sonja. Then you deliberately begin the intricacies of the Dynamos program, step by step as you remember them.

Aha! You've caught his interest. His mind is probing yours again. You're careful to keep all other thoughts out as you think through the long list of numbers and letters.

You keep your head down, as you feel him staring at you from across the table. Then, ever so carefully, you commence the secret lock system program right in the midst of the Dynamos run.

You concentrate as hard as you can, hoping you can recall all of it and that you can hold his attention that long. You watch in astonishment as the man shrinks to his knees in front of you. He falls in a stupor to his feet.

"I think I may have locked his mind," you slowly announce.

THE END

You'll enjoy these Pennypincher novels, too:

CODE RED ON STARSHIP ENGLISIA
Mark A. Durstewitz

Howard, a young communications officer, claims he was rescued from a space accident . . . by an angel of the Lord? In this futuristic tale, Howard must decide whether he is right—or crazy, as the others believe.

42 RED ON FOUR *Nate Aaseng*

Chip won't settle with just being on the football team. He wants to be a starter. But when he achieves his goal, Chip begins to wonder if it's worth it.

THE TRIUMPH *Steve Swanson*

Nothing has gone right for Dave Kendall since his mother died. His relationship with his dad is strained, and both the girl and the car of his dreams seem out of reach. Just when he thinks his dad will never trust him again, Dave is put to the test.

A HORSE NAMED CINNAMON *Jeanne Hovde*

Twelve-year-old Cassie dreams of having her very own riding horse—chestnut colored, fast as the wind. But her dad says there is no money for that. Cassie has to work, and scheme . . . and wait.

DORRIE AND THE MYSTERY OF ANGELL SWAMP
Bonnie Sours Smith

Dorrie Whitfield knows what it's like to be a stranger in Angell. Maybe that's why she feels so deeply for the new French teacher. But what mysteries lurk behind Miss Boyer's solitary walks in Angell Swamp?

VIOLETS GROW IN SECRET PLACES
Marilyn Cram Donahue

Jessica feels like an outsider, living on Bundy Street with no one she can call a friend. Then she meets some people who show her that God's gifts aren't always delivered with a splash, but may grow quietly.

For a complete listing of all Pennypincher titles, write to Chariot Books, 850 N. Grove, Elgin, IL 60120.